FOR ORGANS, PIANOS & ELECTRONIC KEYBOARDS

293

MOVIE CLASSICS

ISBN 978-0-7935-8490-1

HAL•LEONARD®
CORPORATION

7777 W. BLUEMOUND RD. P.O. BOX 13819 MILWAUKEE, WI 53213

Visit Hal Leonard Online at
www.halleonard.com

An Affair to Remember
(Our Love Affair)
from AN AFFAIR TO REMEMBER

Registration 10
Rhythm: Swing

Words by Harold Adamson and Leo McCarey
Music by Harry Warren

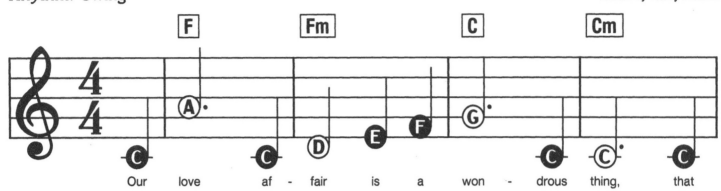

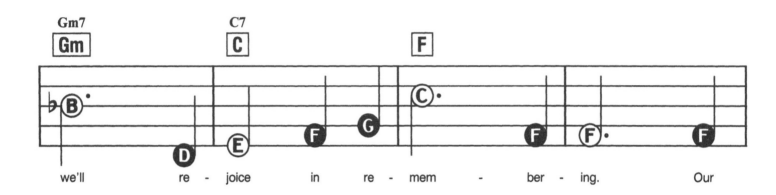

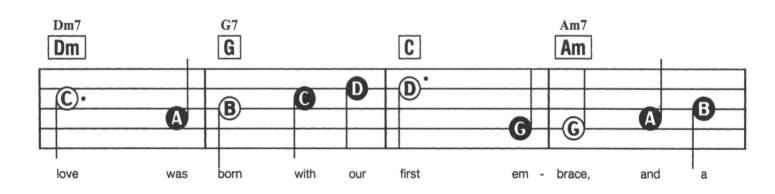

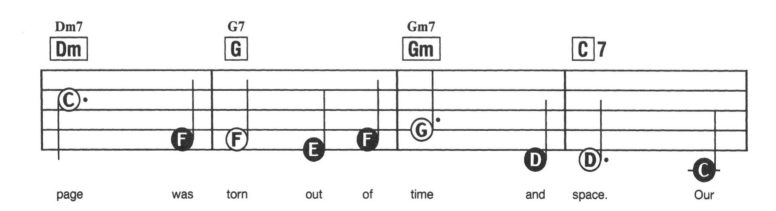

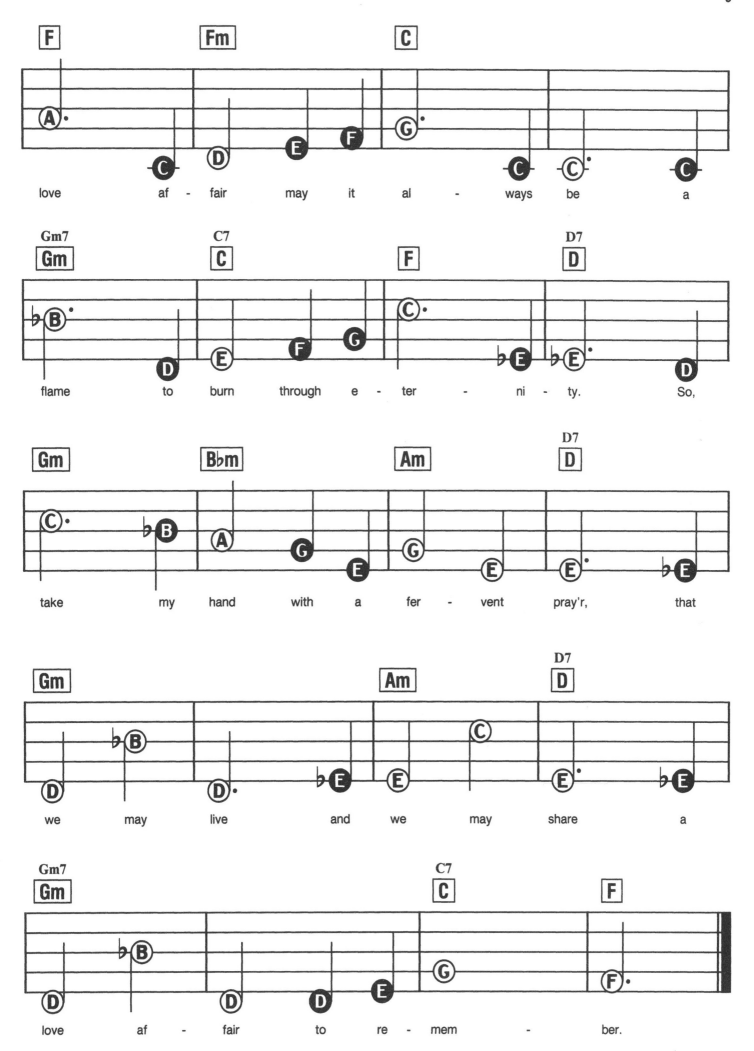

April Love
from APRIL LOVE

Registration 9
Rhythm: Swing

Words by Paul Francis Webster
Music by Sammy Fain

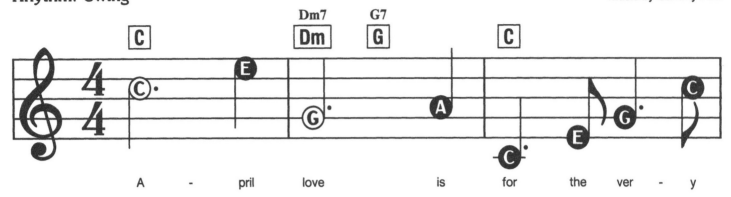

A - pril love is for the ver - y

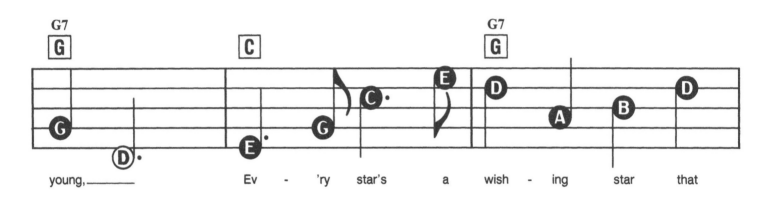

young, _____ Ev - 'ry star's a wish - ing star that

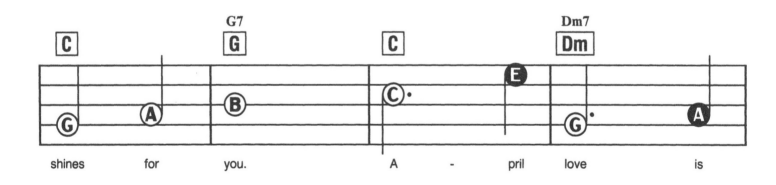

shines for you. A - pril love is

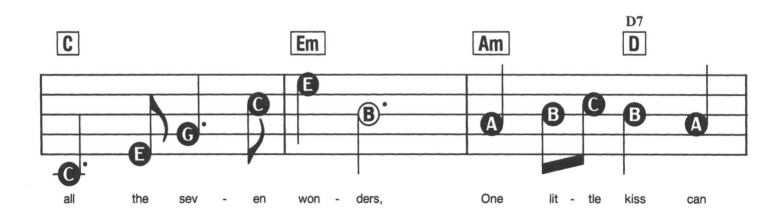

all the sev - en won - ders, One lit - tle kiss can

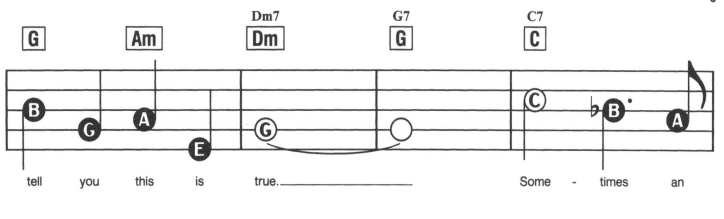

tell you this is true._____ Some - times an

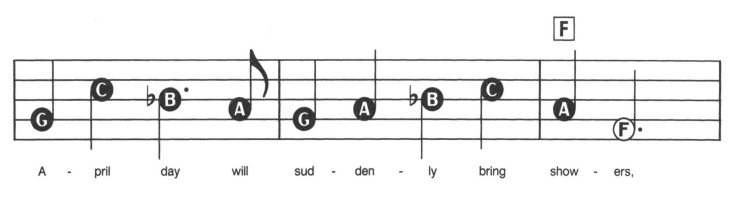

A - pril day will sud - den - ly bring show - ers,

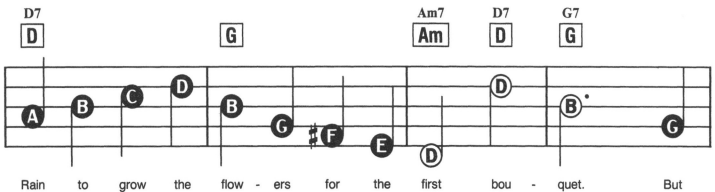

Rain to grow the flow - ers for the first bou - quet. But

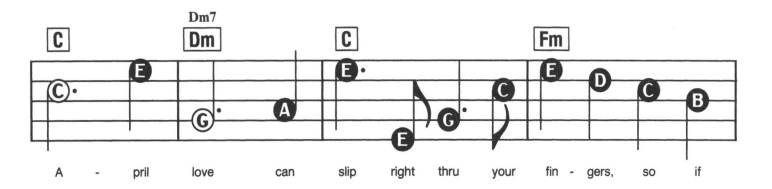

A - pril love can slip right thru your fin - gers, so if

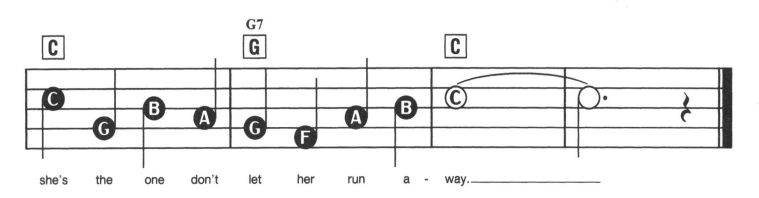

she's the one don't let her run a - way._____

Buttons and Bows
from the Paramount Picture PALEFACE

Registration 4
Rhythm: Swing

Words and Music by Jay Livingston
and Ray Evans

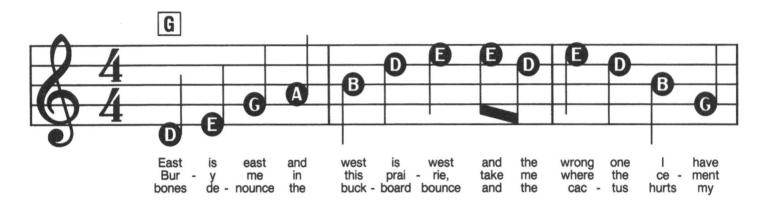

East is east and west is west and the wrong one I have
Bur - y me in this prai - rie, take me where the ce - ment
bones de - nounce the buck - board bounce and the cac - tus hurts my

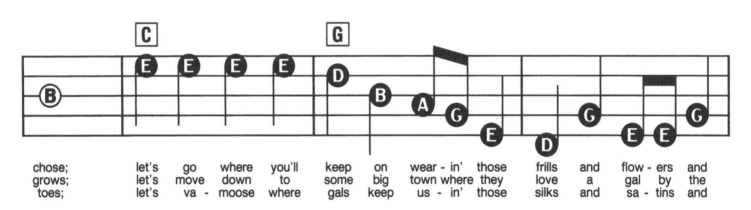

chose; let's go where you'll keep on wear - in' those frills and flow - ers and
grows; let's move down to some big town where they love a gal by the
toes; let's va - moose where some gals keep us - in' those silks and sa - tins and

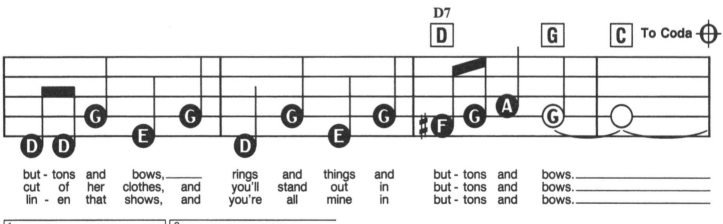

but - tons and bows,_____ rings and things and you'll stand out in but - tons and bows._____
cut of her clothes, and you're all mine in but - tons and bows._____
lin - en that shows, and

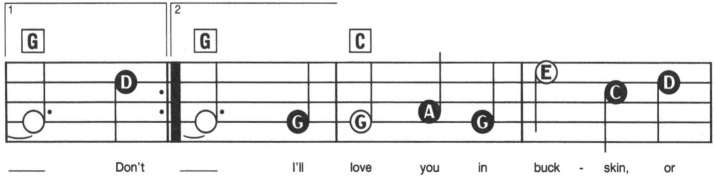

Don't _____ I'll love you in buck - skin, or

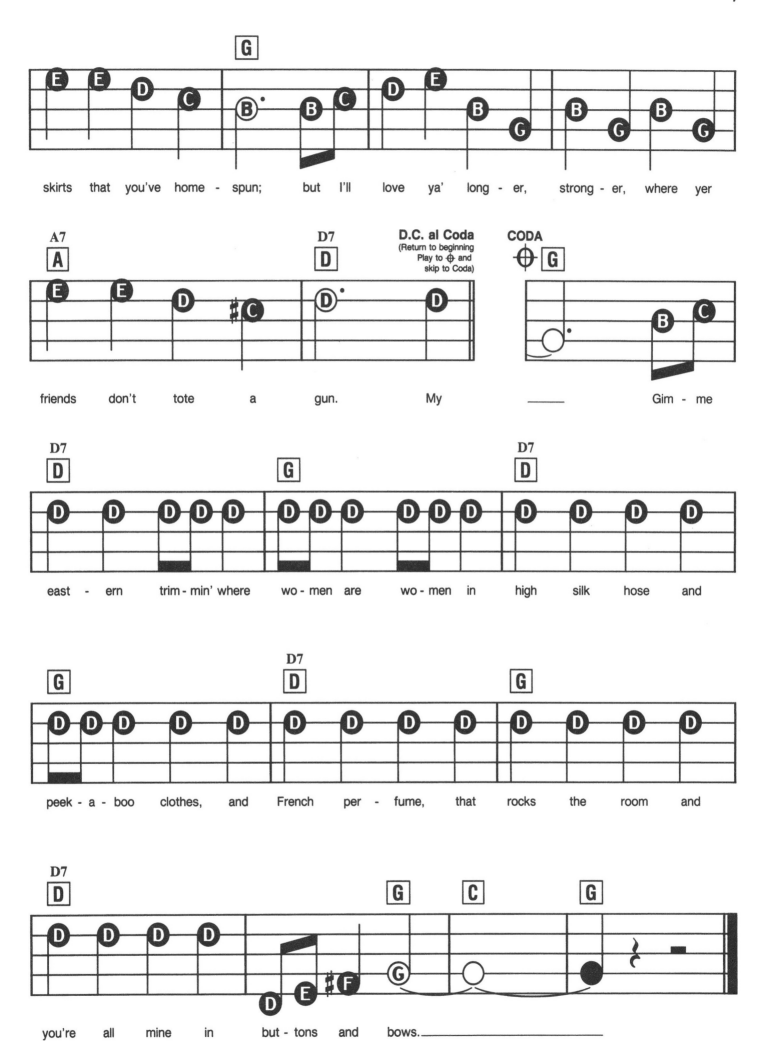

Call Me Irresponsible
from the Paramount Picture PAPA'S DELICATE CONDITION

Registration 7
Rhythm: Swing or Big Band

Words by Sammy Cahn
Music by James Van Heusen

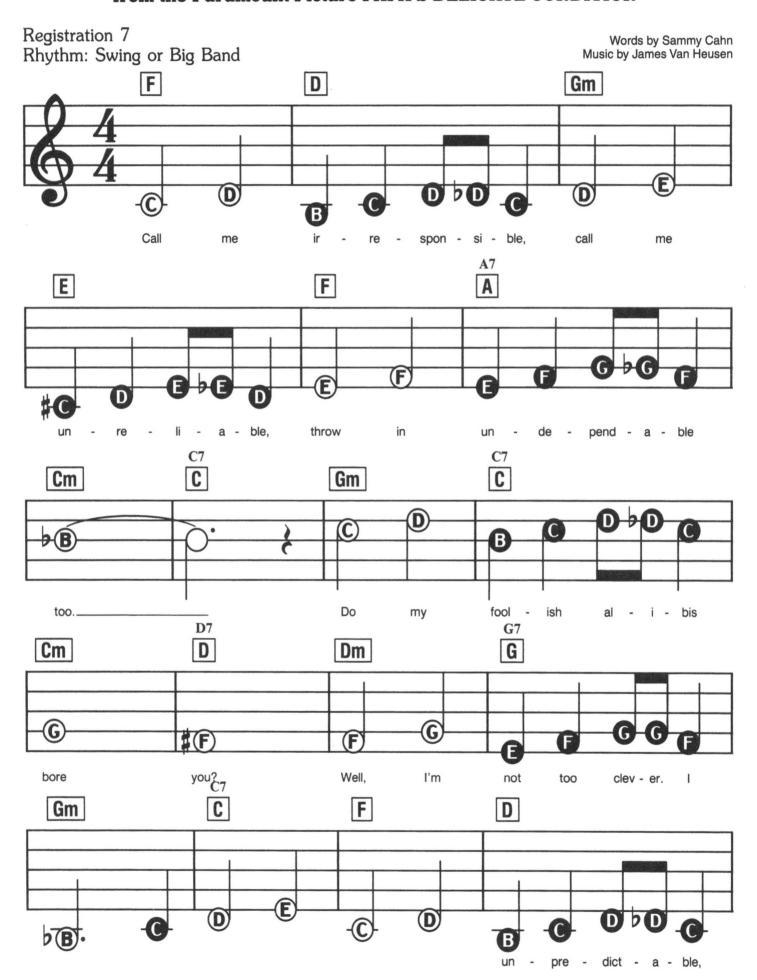

9

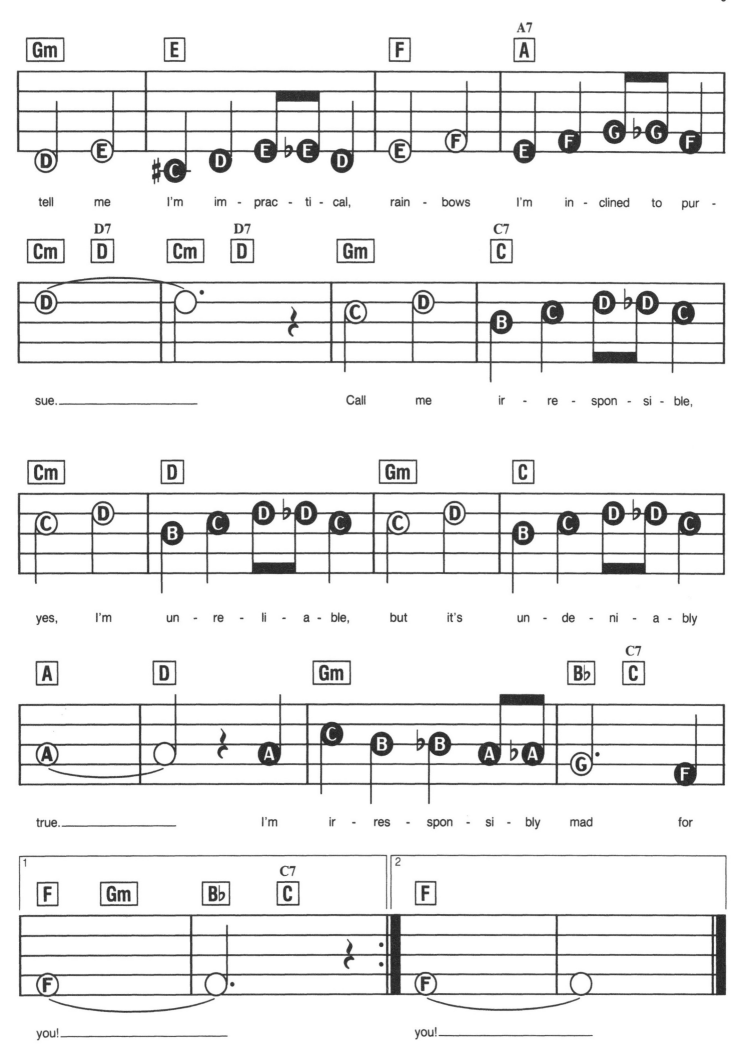

A Certain Smile
from A CERTAIN SMILE

Registration 2
Rhythm: Swing

Words by Paul Francis Webster
Music by Sammy Fain

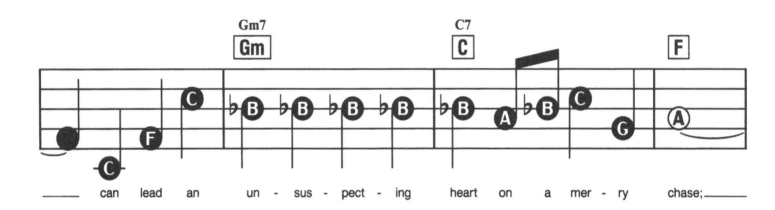

A cer - tain smile,_____ a cer - tain face,_____

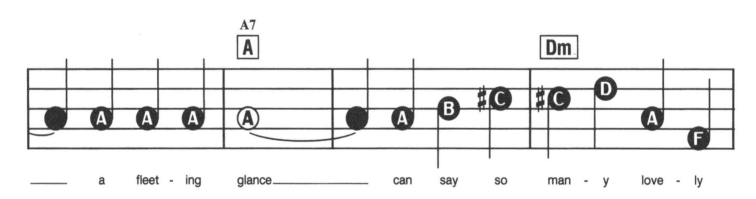

_____ can lead an un - sus - pect - ing heart on a mer - ry chase;_____

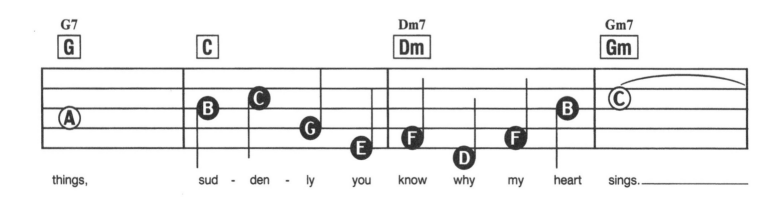

_____ a fleet - ing glance_____ can say so man - y love - ly

things, sud - den - ly you know why my heart sings._____

11

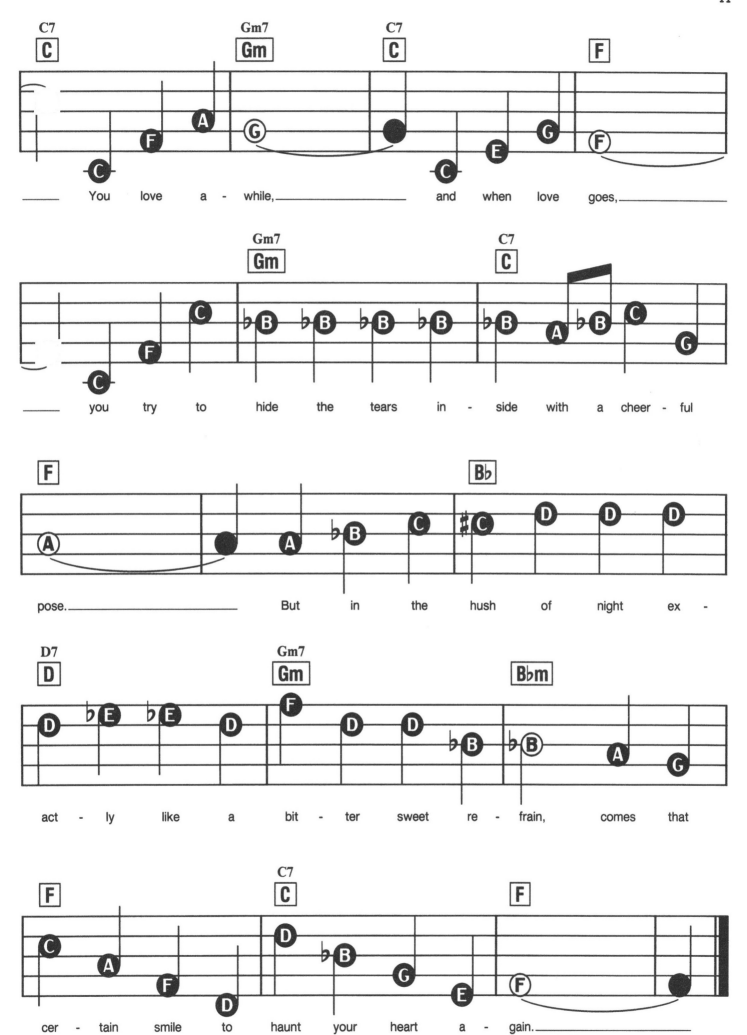

Charade
from CHARADE

Registration 3
Rhythm: Waltz

Music by Henry Mancini
Words by Johnny Mercer

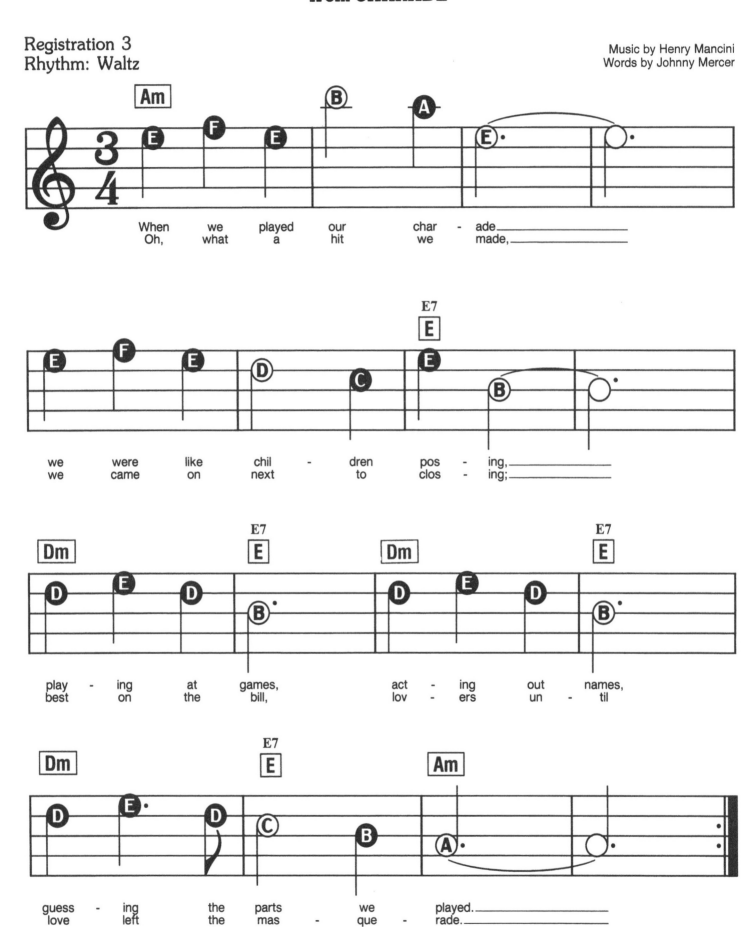

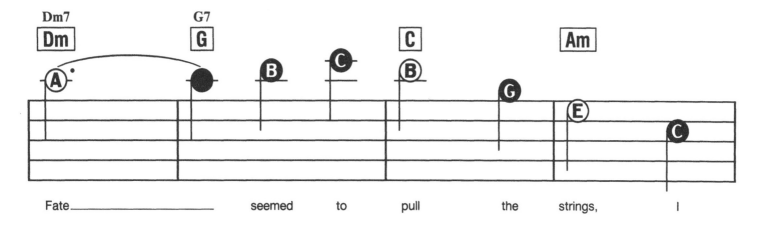

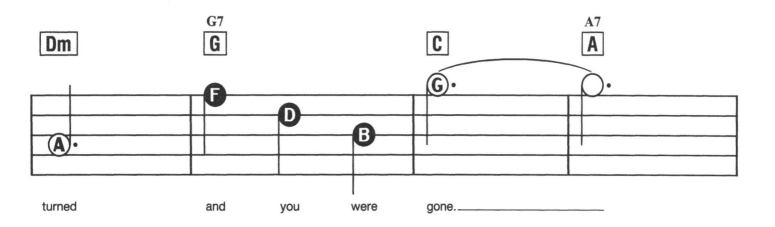

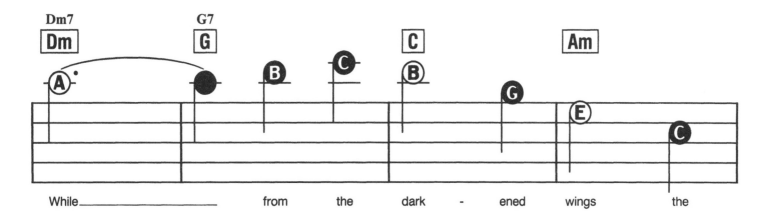

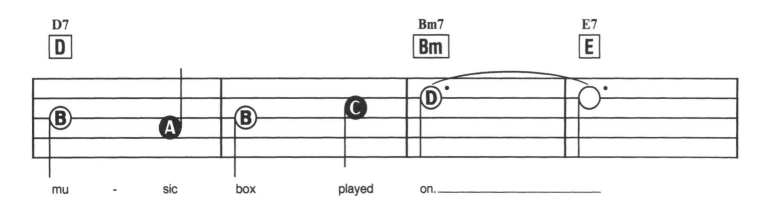

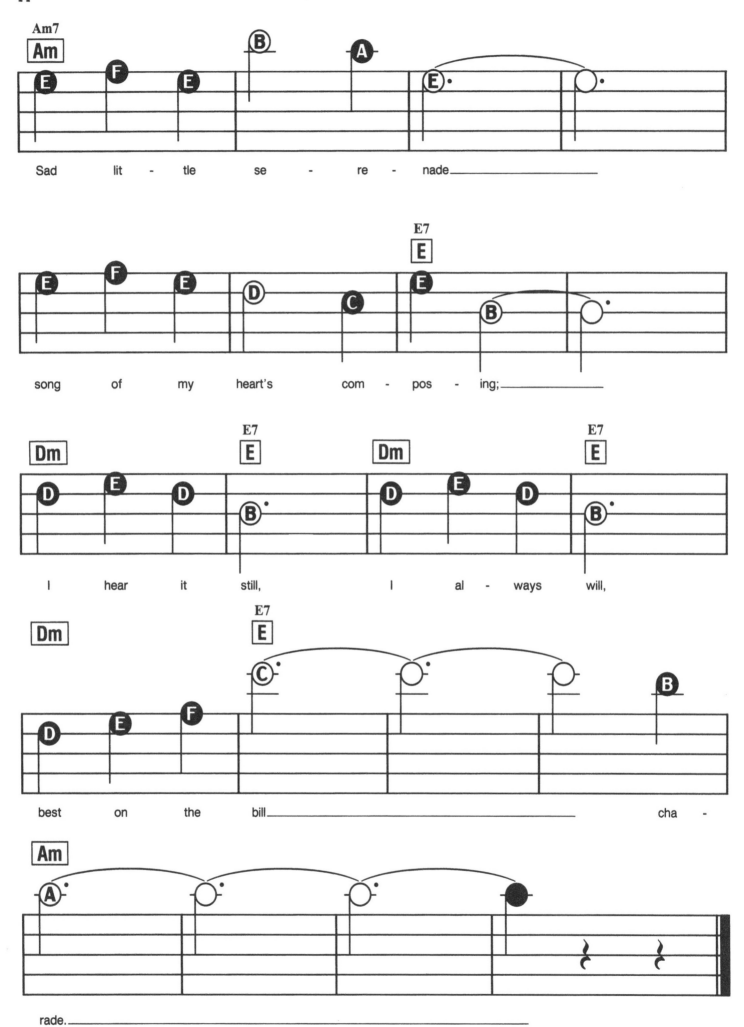

Dear Heart
from DEAR HEART

Registration 3
Rhythm: Waltz

Music by Henry Mancini
Words by Jay Livingston and Ray Evans

F		F7 / F		
A.	C.	D	C	A
Dear	heart,	wish	you	were

Bb	F	G7 / G
F	D	C. A.
here	to warm	this

Gm7 / Gm	C7 / C	F
G.	○ #G	A.
night._____	My	dear

	F7 / F	Bb
C.	D C. A	F D
heart,	seems like a year	since

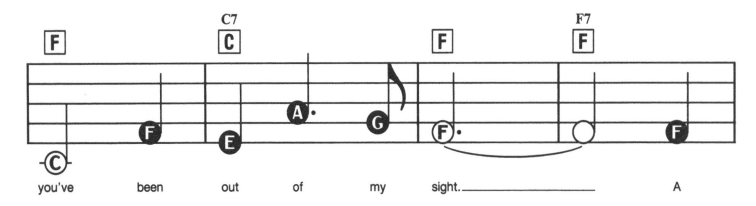

you've been out of my sight._____ A

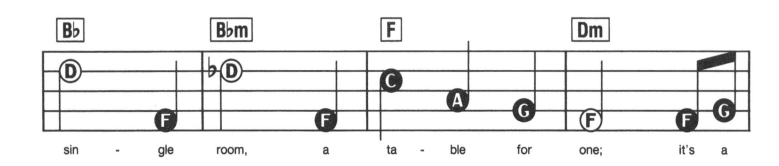

sin - gle room, a ta - ble for one; it's a

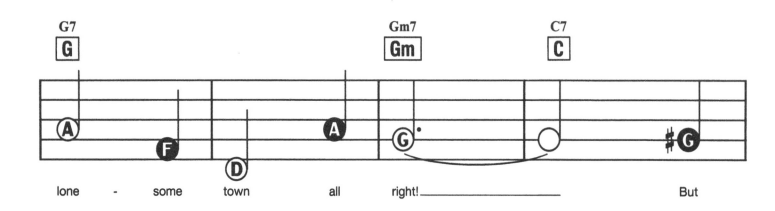

lone - some town all right!_____ But

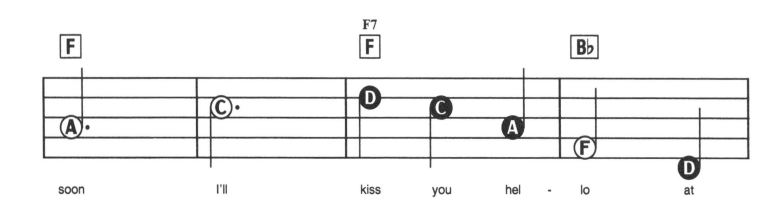

soon I'll kiss you hel - lo at

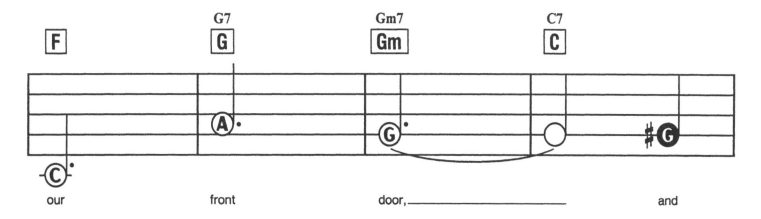

our   front   door,_____   and

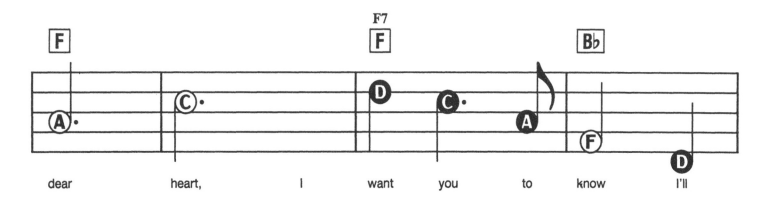

dear   heart,   I   want   you   to   know   I'll

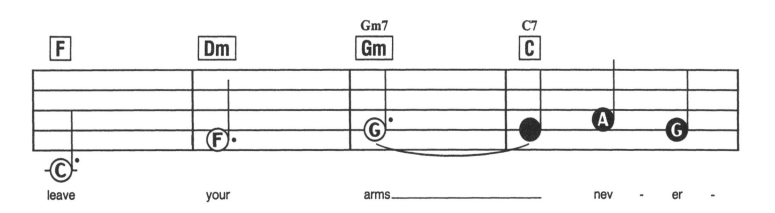

leave   your   arms_____   nev -   er -

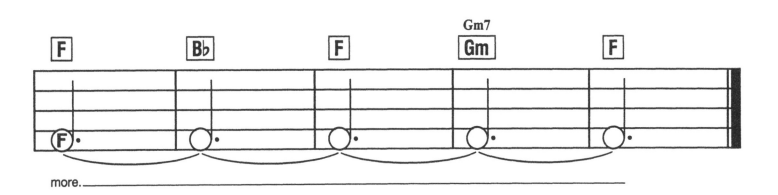

more._____

The Hands of Time
Theme from the Screen Gems Television Production BRIAN'S SONG

Registration 3
Rhythm: Pops or 8 Beat

Words by Alan and Marilyn Bergman
Music by Michel Legrand

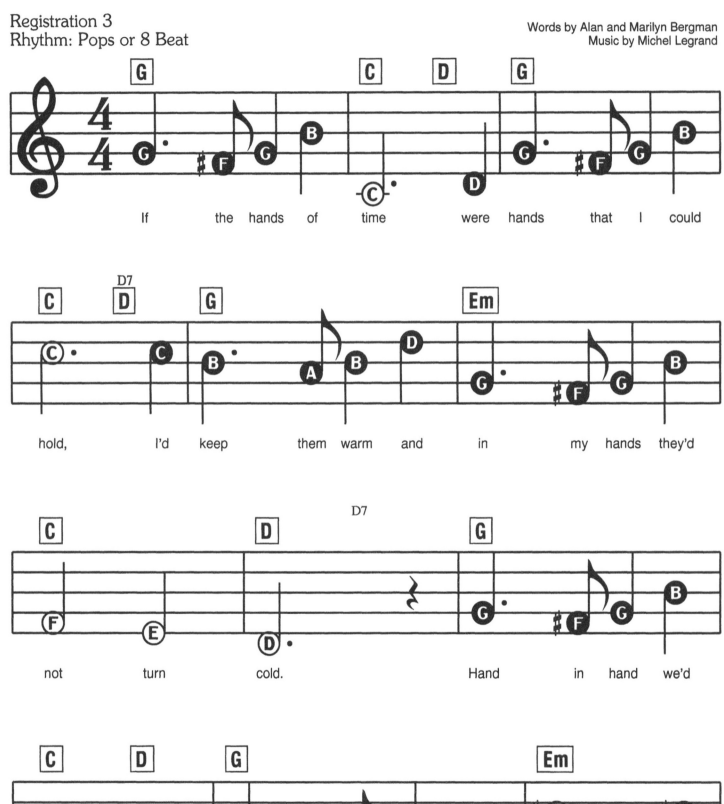

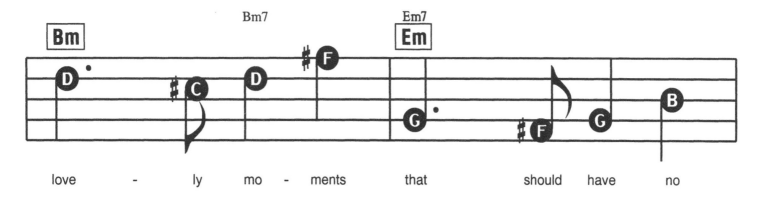

love - ly mo - ments that should have no

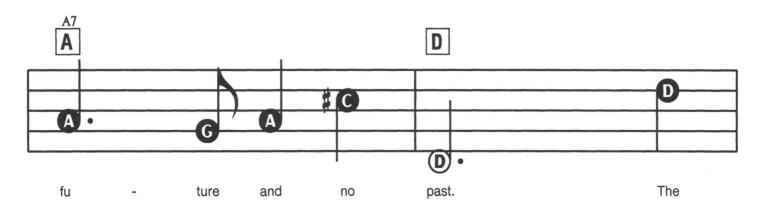

fu - ture and no past. The

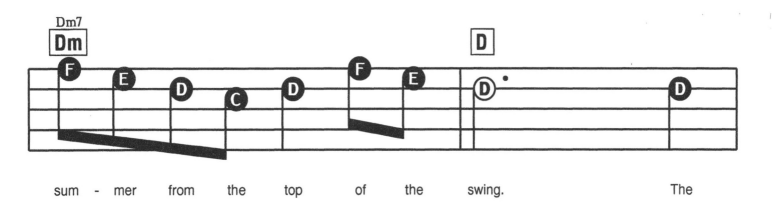

sum - mer from the top of the swing. The

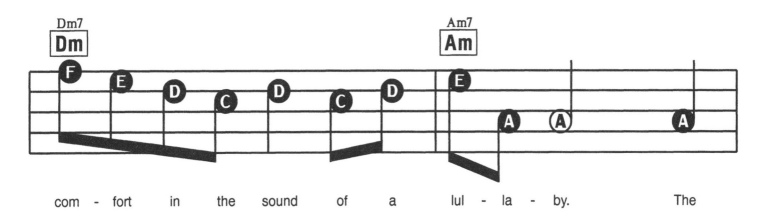

com - fort in the sound of a lul - la - by. The

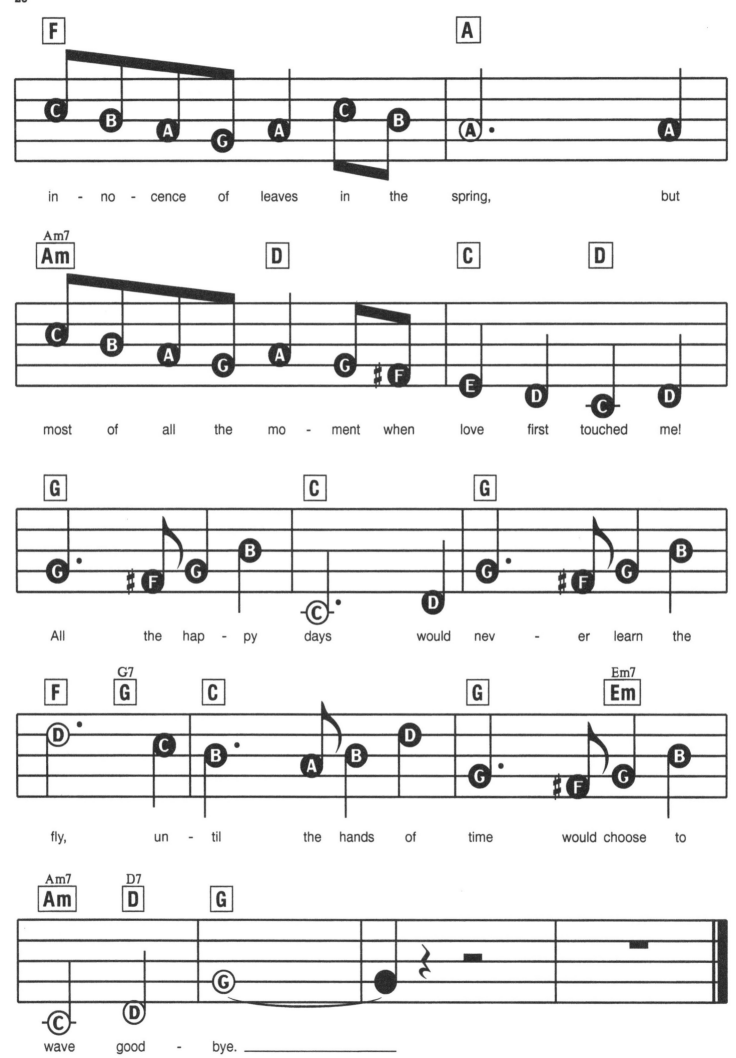

Theme from "Ice Castles"
(Through the Eyes of Love)
from ICE CASTLES

Registration 1
Rhythm: Slow Rock or Ballad

Lyrics by Carole Bayer Sager
Music by Marvin Hamlisch

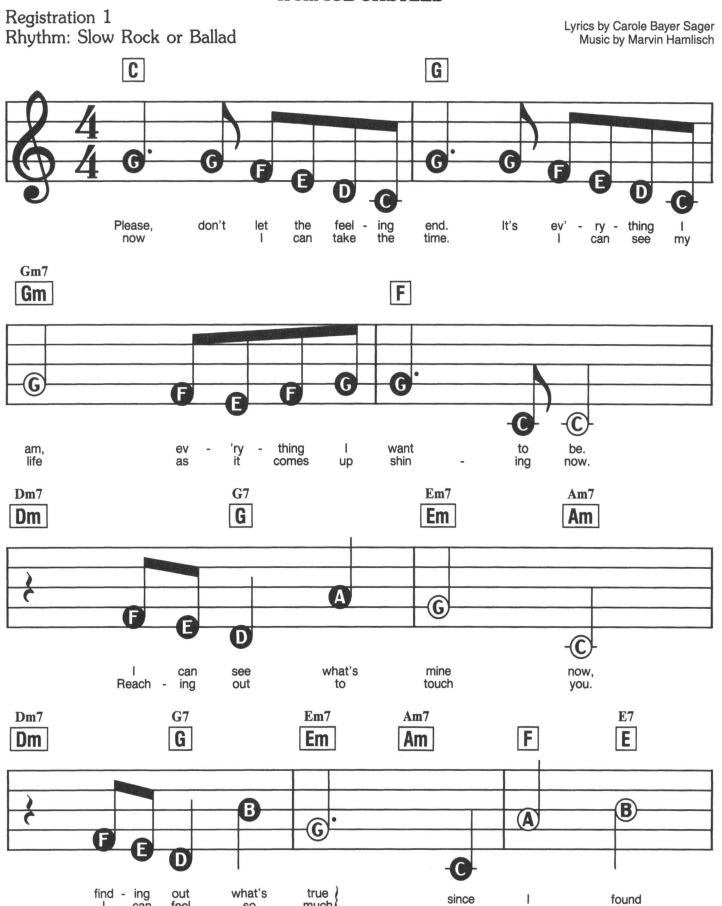

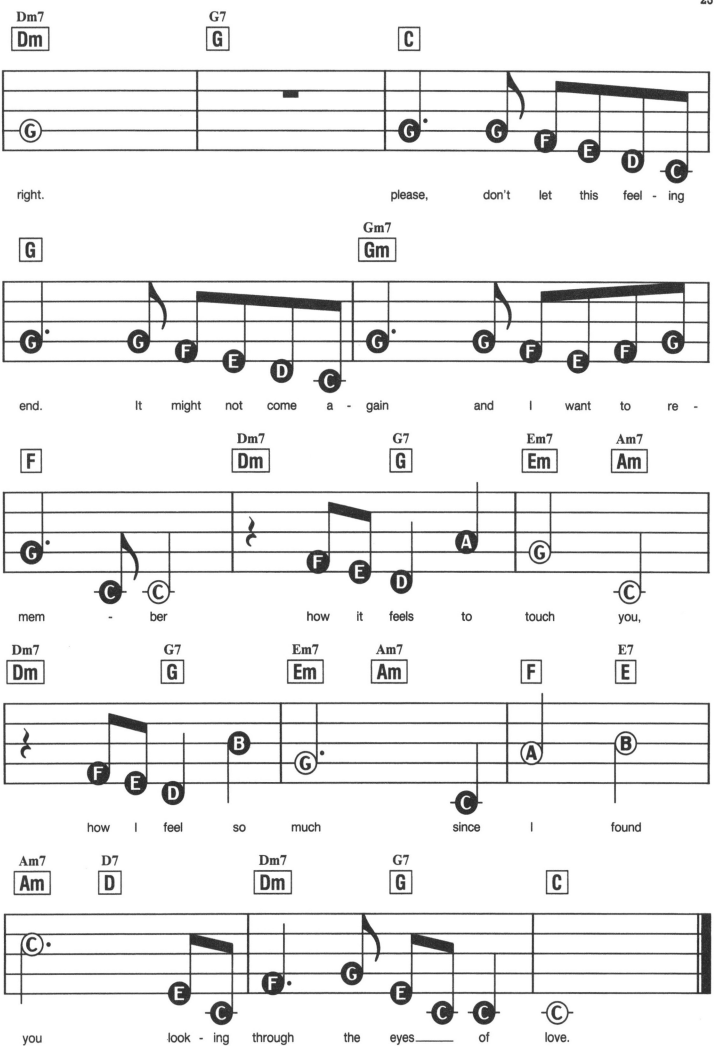

Theme from "Lawrence Of Arabia"
from LAWRENCE OF ARABIA

Registration 5
Rhythm: Ballad

By Maurice Jarre

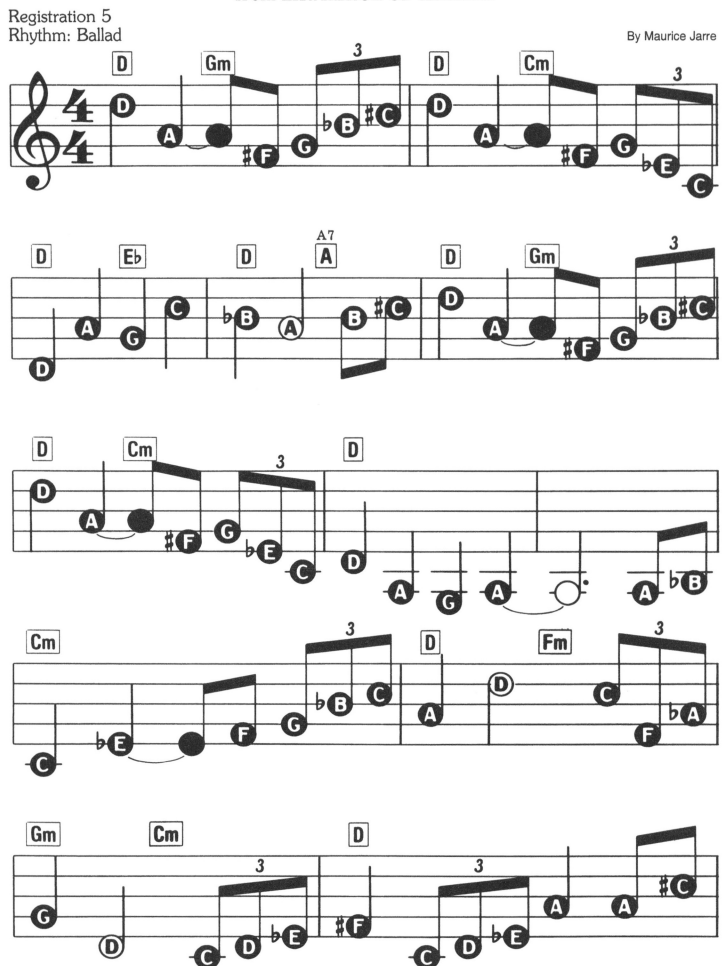

Love Is a Many-Splendored Thing

from LOVE IS A MANY-SPLENDORED THING

Registration 9
Rhythm: Swing

Words by Paul Francis Webster
Music by Sammy Fain

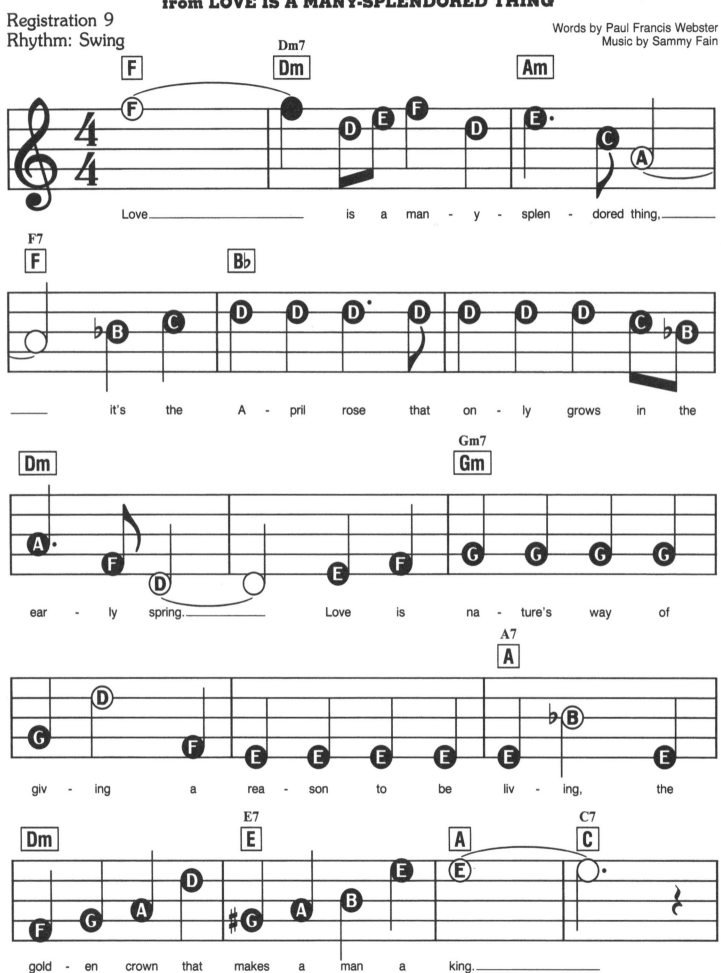

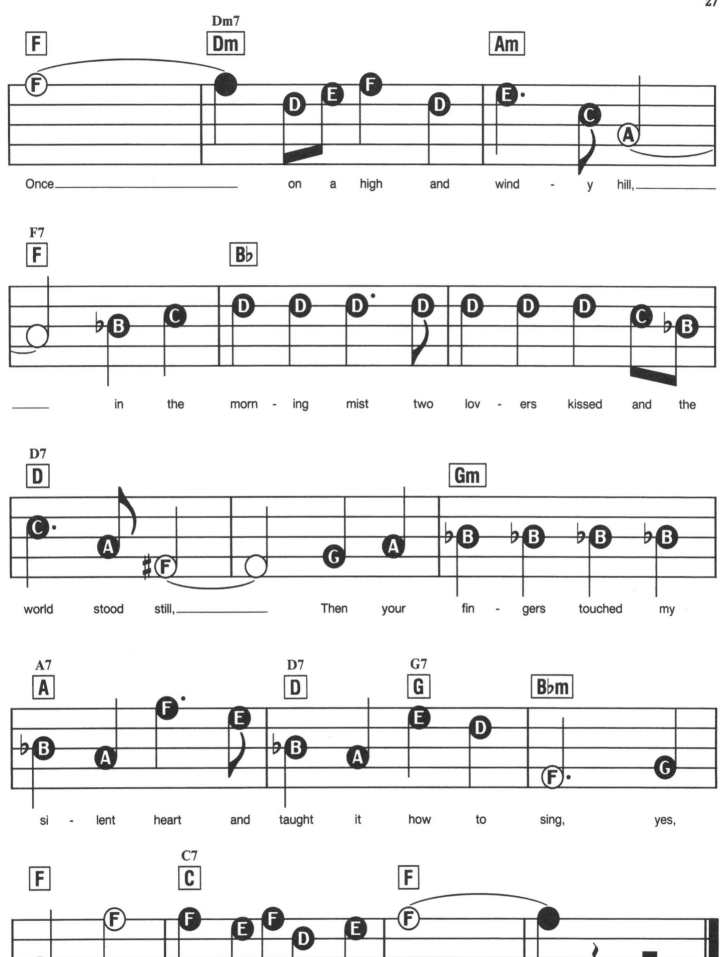

Midnight Cowboy
from the Motion Picture MIDNIGHT COWBOY

Registration 1
Rhythm: Slow Rock

By John Barry

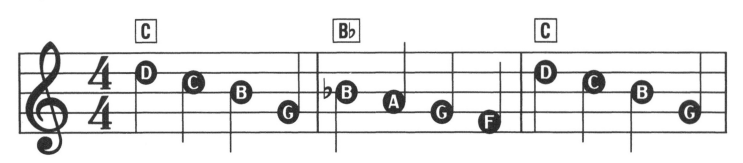

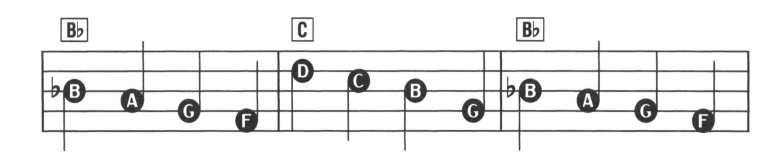

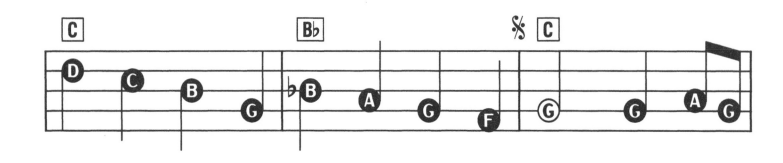

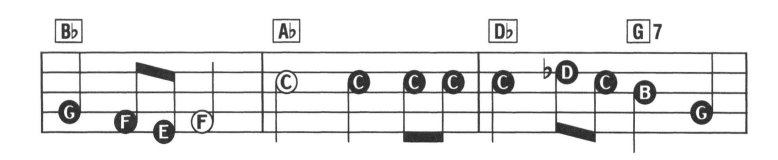

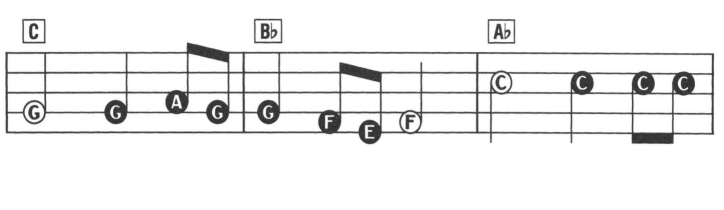

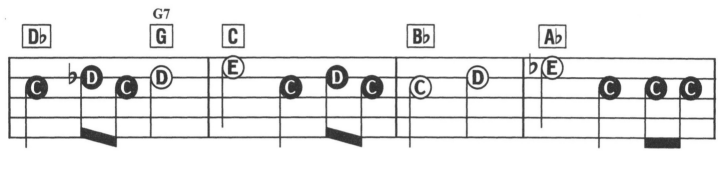

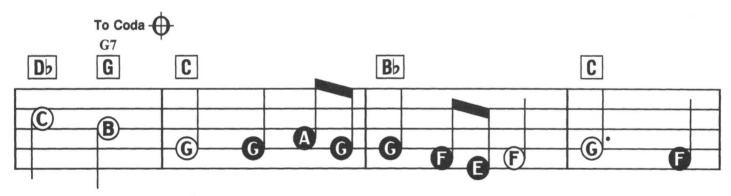

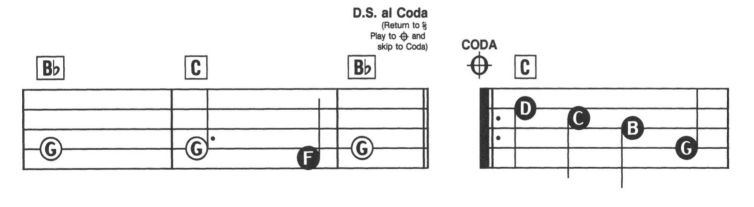

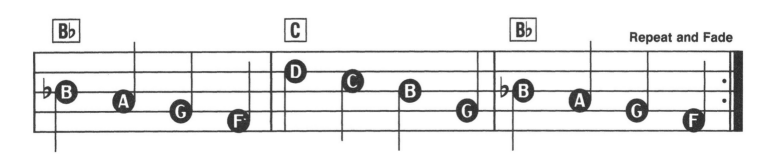

Moon River
from the Paramount Picture BREAKFAST AT TIFFANY'S

Registration 3
Rhythm: Waltz

Words by Johnny Mercer
Music by Henry Mancini

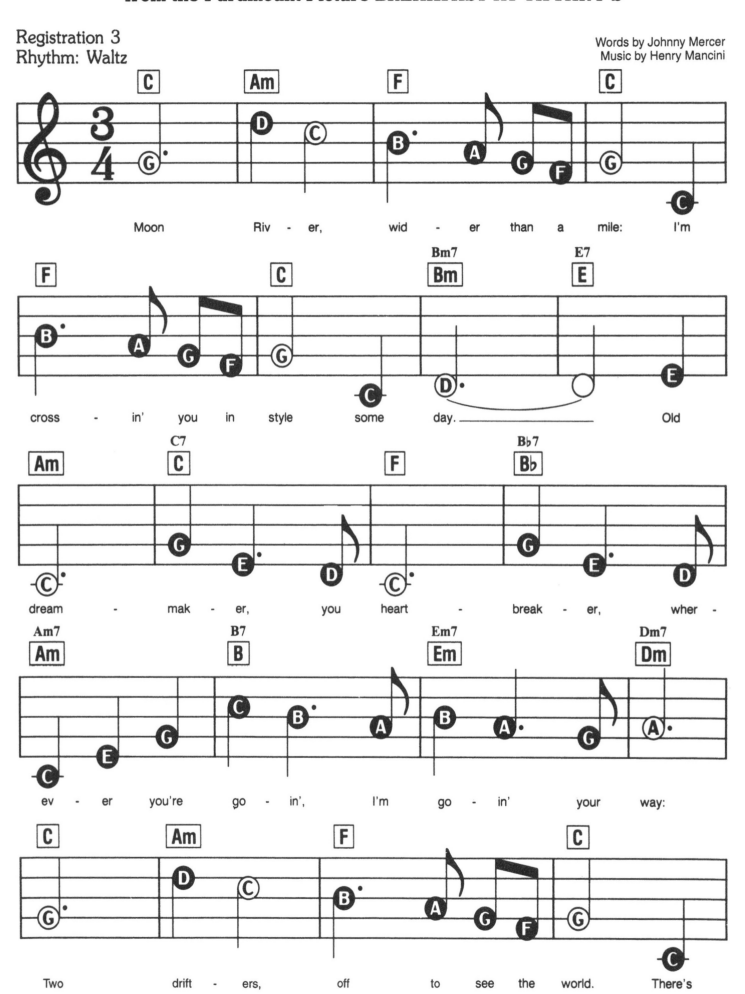

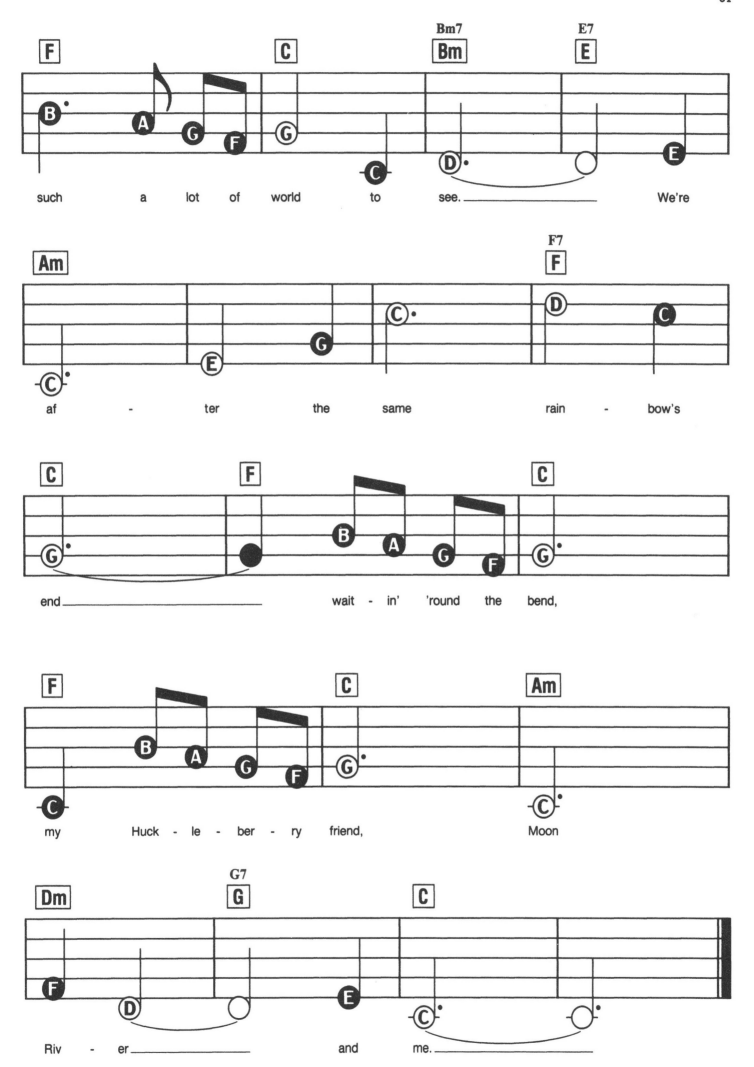

Nobody Does It Better

from THE SPY WHO LOVED ME

Registration 4
Rhythm: Ballad or Rock

Lyrics by Carole Bayer Sager
Music by Marvin Hamlisch

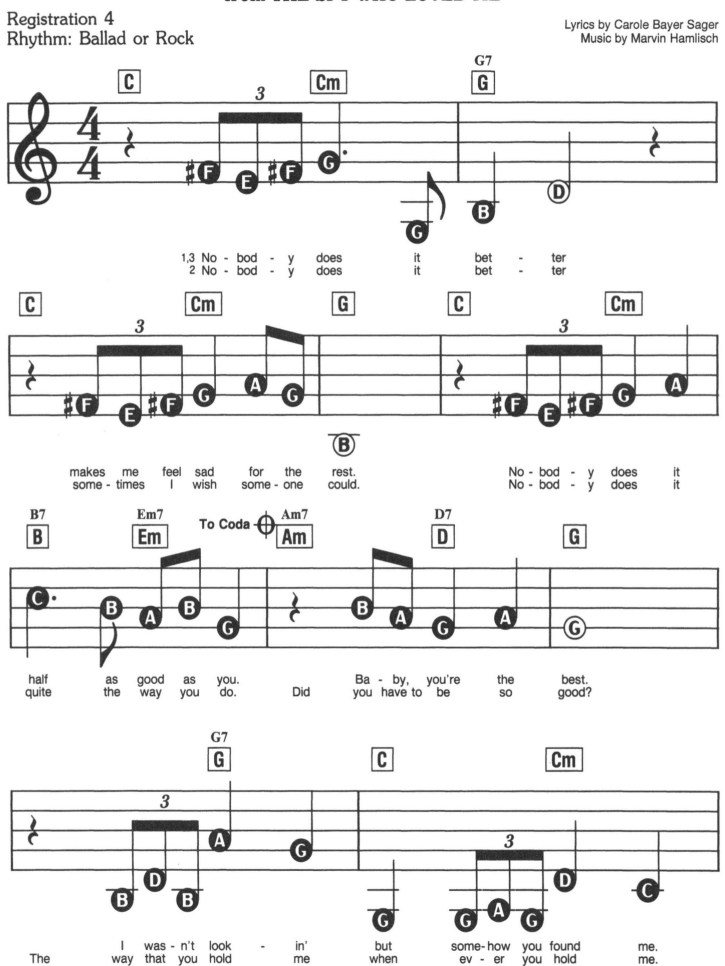

New York, New York

from NEW YORK, NEW YORK

Registration 4
Rhythm: Swing

Music by John Kander
Words by Fred Ebb

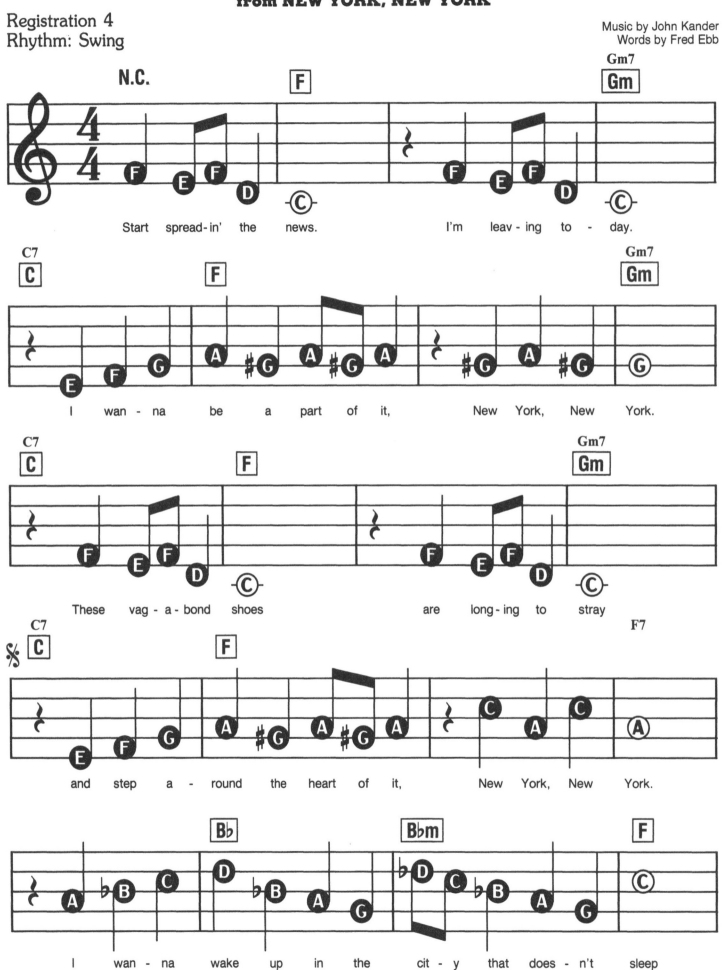

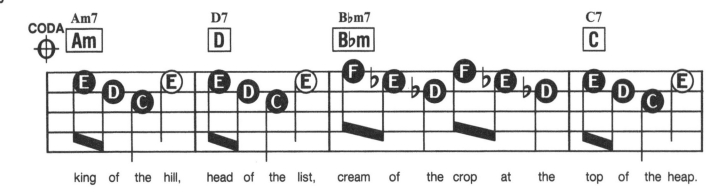

king of the hill, head of the list, cream of the crop at the top of the heap.

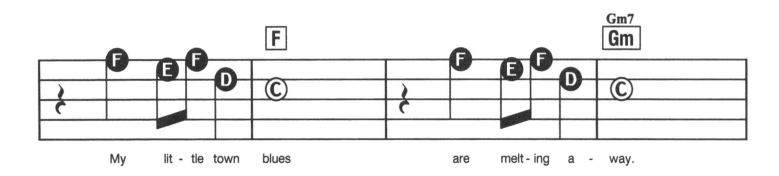

My lit - tle town blues are melt - ing a - way.

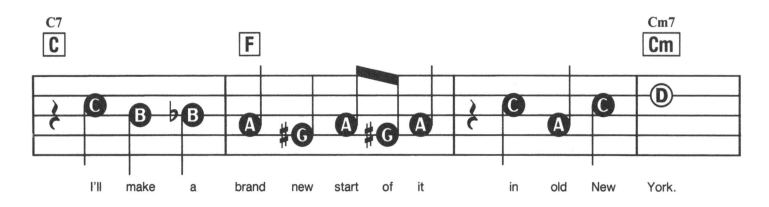

I'll make a brand new start of it in old New York.

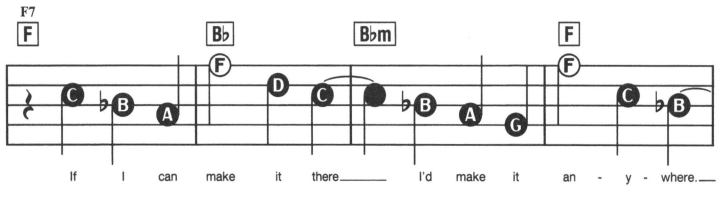

If I can make it there___ I'd make it an - y - where.___

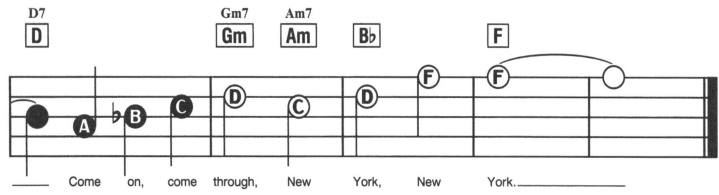

Come on, come through, New York, New York.___

Over the Rainbow
from THE WIZARD OF OZ

Registration 5
Rhythm: Fox Trot or Swing

Lyric by E.Y. Harburg
Music by Harold Arlen

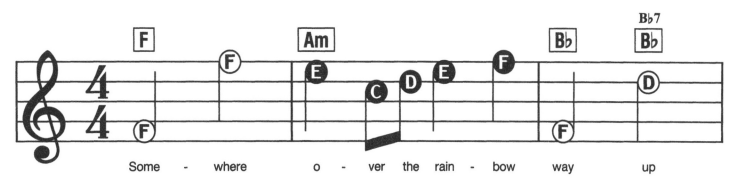

Some - where   o - ver the rain - bow   way   up

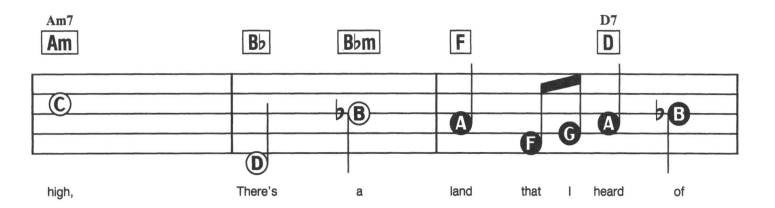

high,   There's   a   land   that   I   heard   of

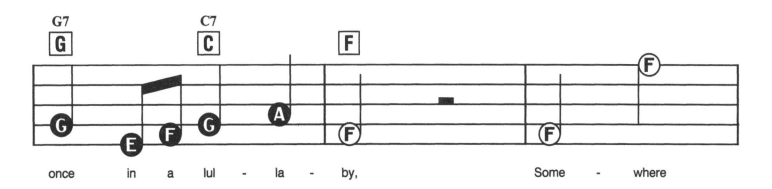

once   in   a   lul - la - by,   Some - where

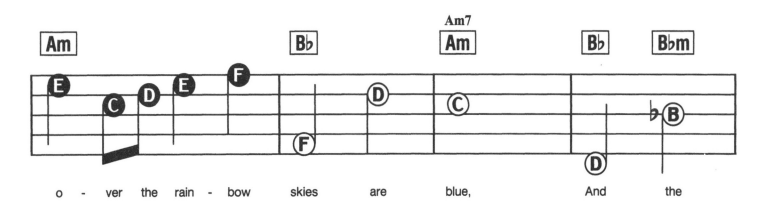

o - ver   the   rain - bow   skies   are   blue,   And   the

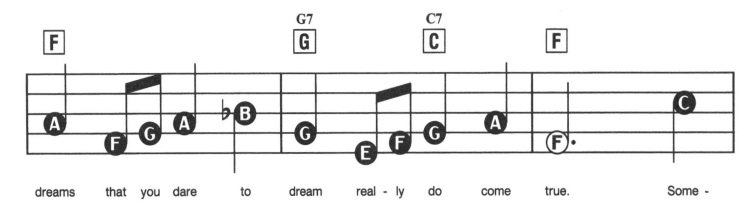

dreams that you dare to dream real - ly do come true. Some -

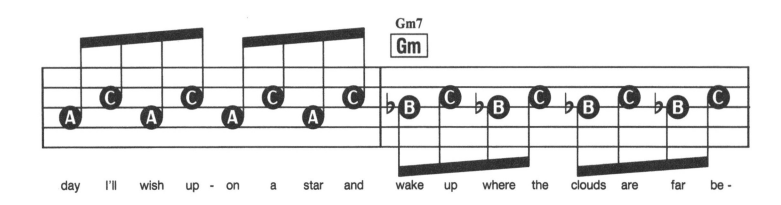

day I'll wish up - on a star and wake up where the clouds are far be -

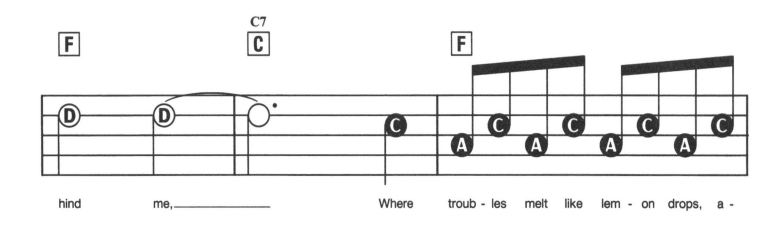

hind me,_____ Where troub - les melt like lem - on drops, a -

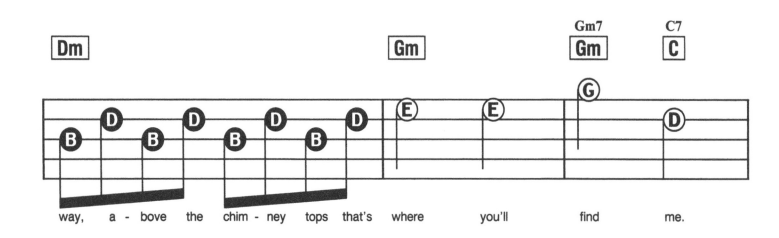

way, a - bove the chim - ney tops that's where you'll find me.

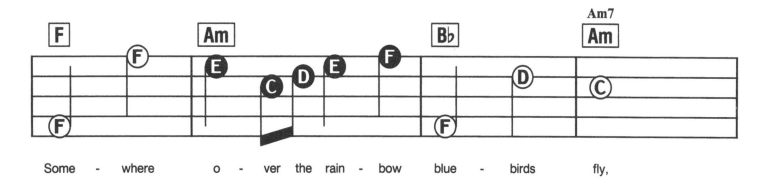

Some - where   o - ver   the rain - bow   blue - birds   fly,

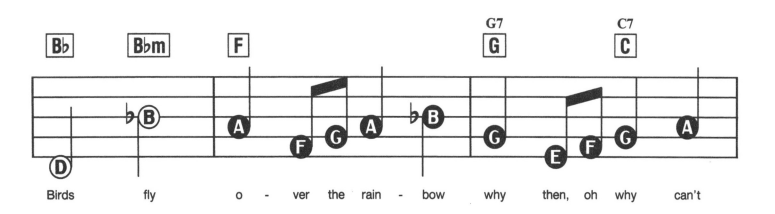

Birds   fly   o - ver   the rain - bow   why   then, oh   why   can't

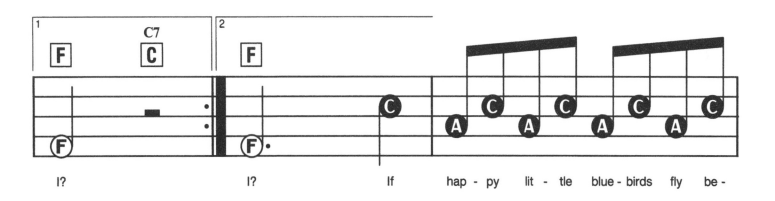

I?   I?   If   hap - py   lit - tle   blue - birds   fly   be -

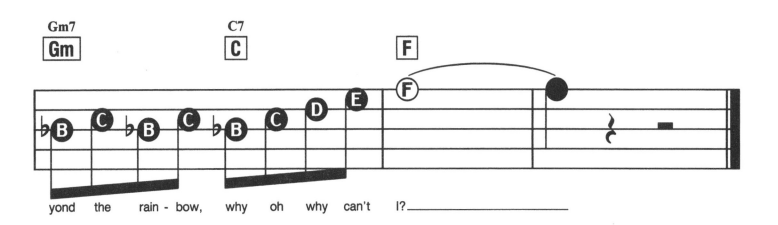

yond   the   rain - bow,   why   oh   why   can't   I?

On the Atchison, Topeka and the Santa Fe

from THE HARVEY GIRLS

Registration 9
Rhythm: Swing

Words by Johnny Mercer
Music by Harry Warren

The Pink Panther
from THE PINK PANTHER

Registration 7
Rhythm: Swing

By Henry Mancini

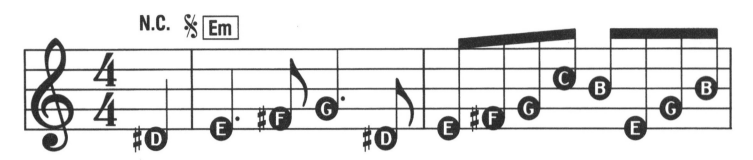

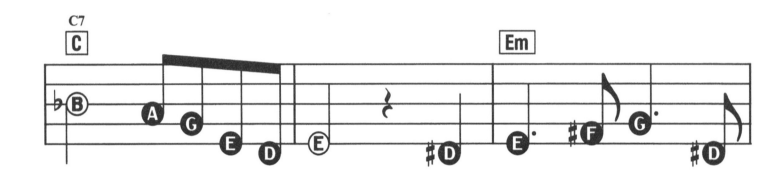

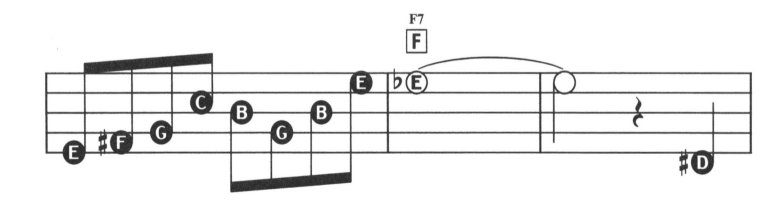

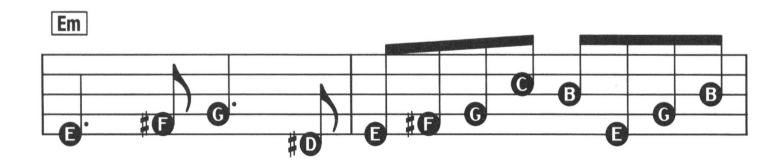

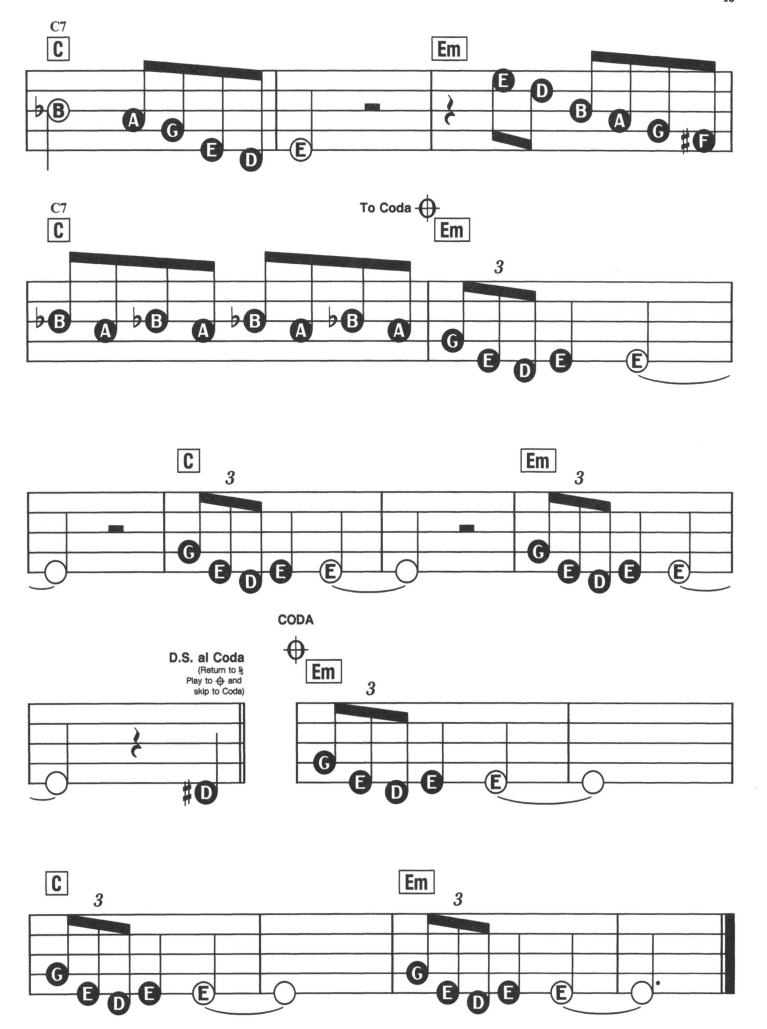

The Shadow of Your Smile
Love Theme from THE SANDPIPER

Registration 4
Rhythm: Bossa Nova or Latin

Lyric by Paul Francis Webster
Music by Johnny Mandel

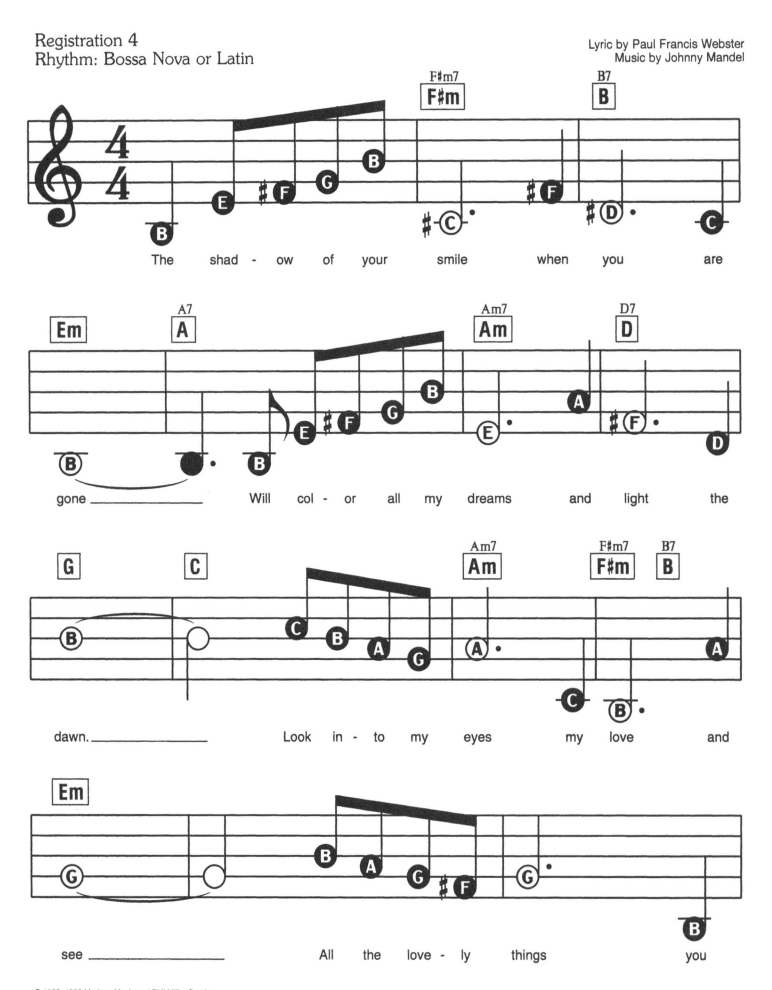

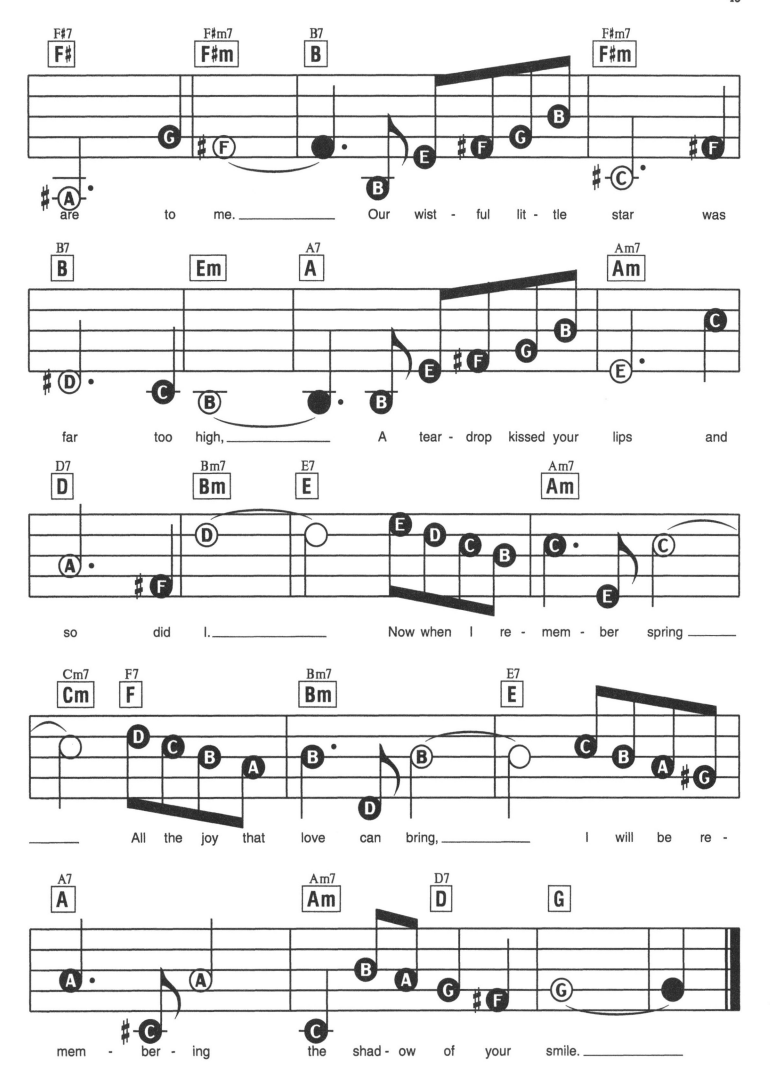

Singin' in the Rain

from SINGIN' IN THE RAIN

Registration 4
Rhythm: Swing

Words by Arthur Freed
Music by Nacio Herb Brown

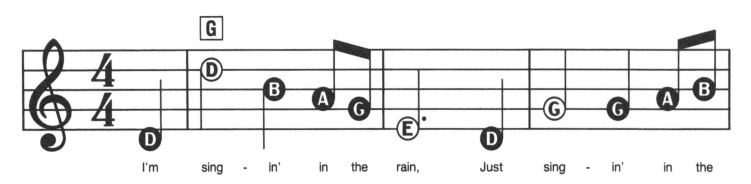

I'm sing - in' in the rain, Just sing - in' in the

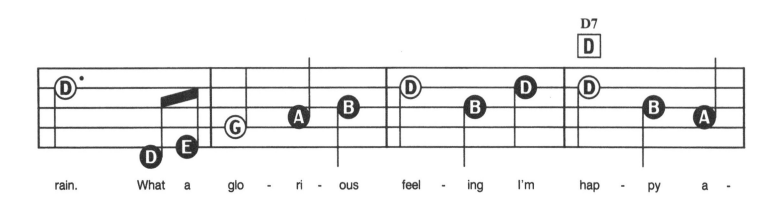

rain. What a glo - ri - ous feel - ing I'm hap - py a -

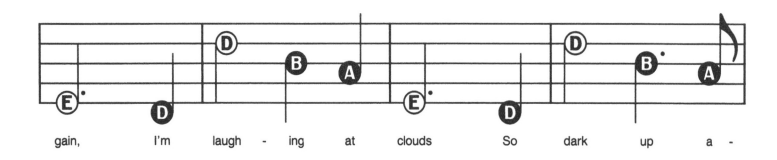

gain, I'm laugh - ing at clouds So dark up a -

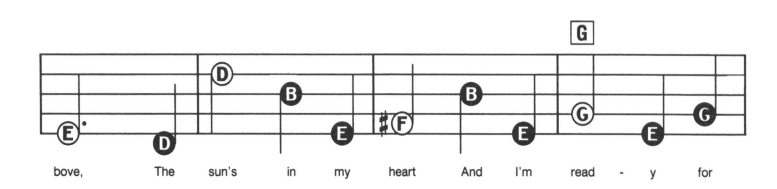

bove, The sun's in my heart And I'm read - y for

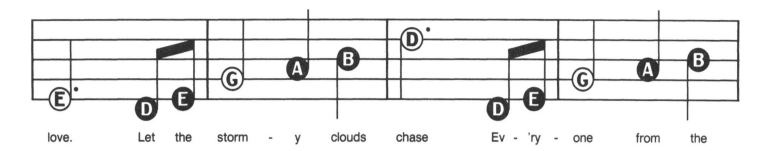

love.   Let   the   storm - y   clouds   chase   Ev - 'ry - one   from   the

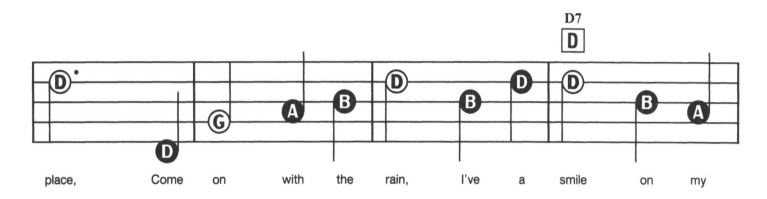

place,   Come   on   with   the   rain,   I've   a   smile   on   my

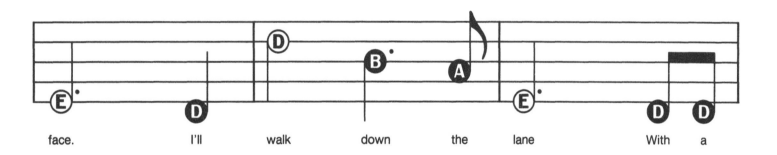

face.   I'll   walk   down   the   lane   With   a

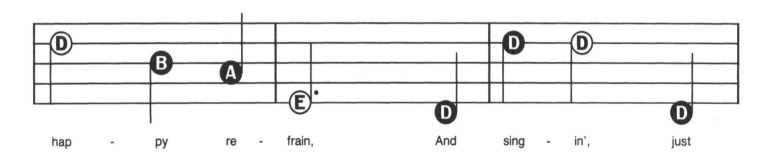

hap - py   re - frain,   And   sing - in',   just

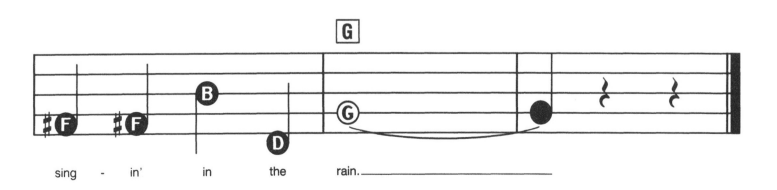

sing - in'   in   the   rain. _____

Somewhere, My Love
Lara's Theme from DOCTOR ZHIVAGO

Registration 9
Rhythm: Waltz

Lyric by Paul Francis Webster
Music by Maurice Jarre

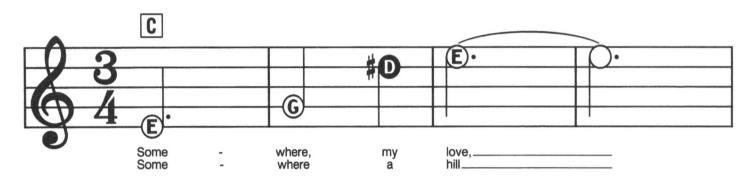

Some - where, my love,_____
Some - where a hill_____

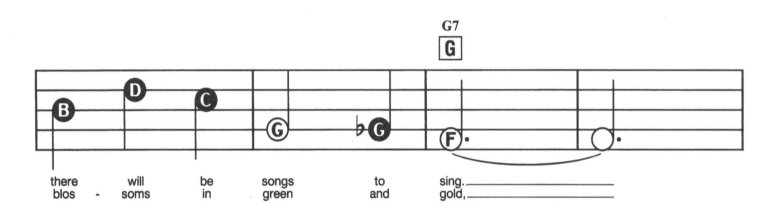

there will be songs to sing._____
blos - soms in green and gold,_____

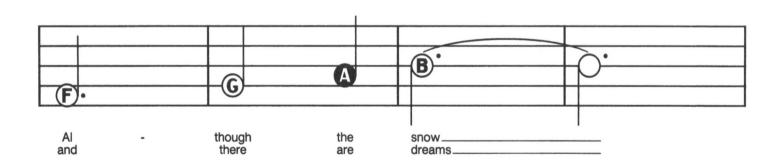

Al - though the snow_____
and there are dreams_____

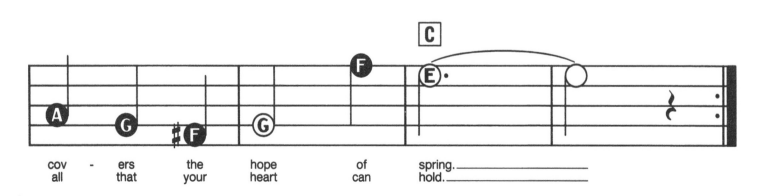

cov - ers the hope of spring._____
all that your heart can hold._____

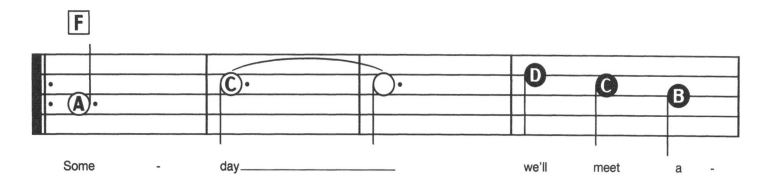

Some - day_____ we'll meet a -

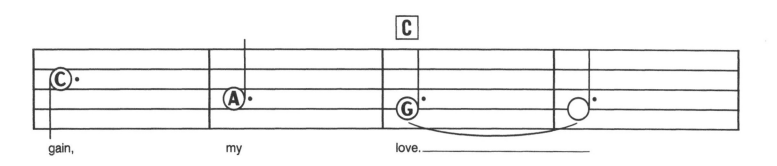

gain, my love._____

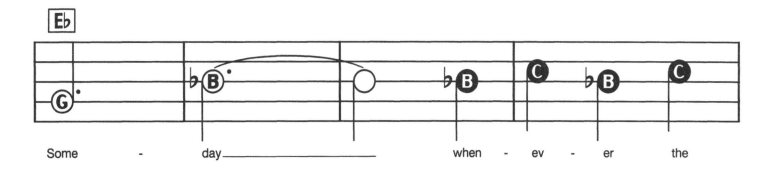

Some - day_____ when - ev - er the

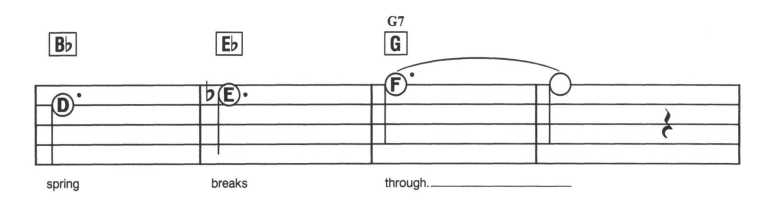

spring breaks through._____

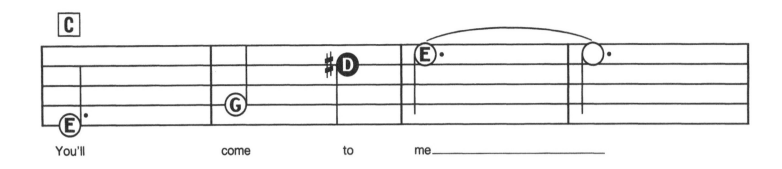

You'll come to me

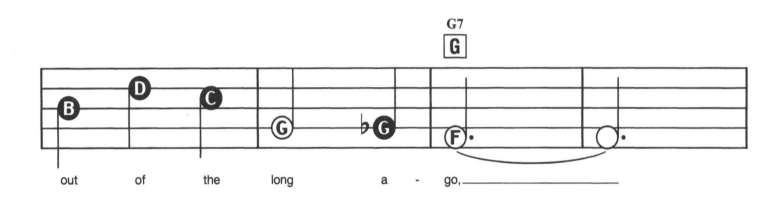

out of the long a - go,

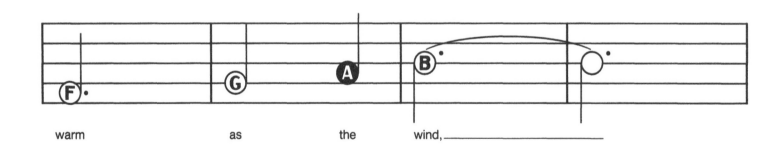

warm as the wind,

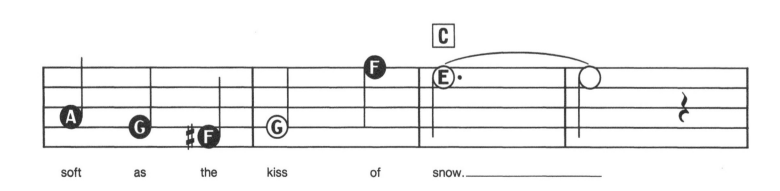

soft as the kiss of snow.

51

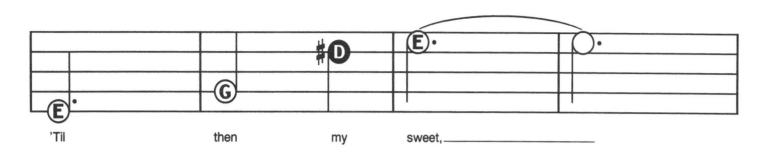

'Til   then   my   sweet,_____

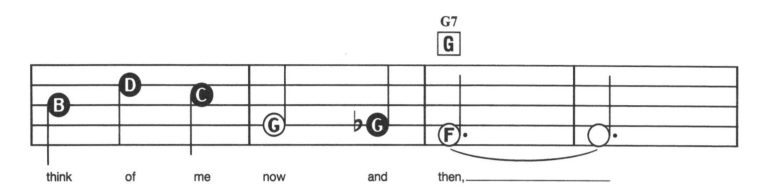

think   of   me   now   and   then,_____

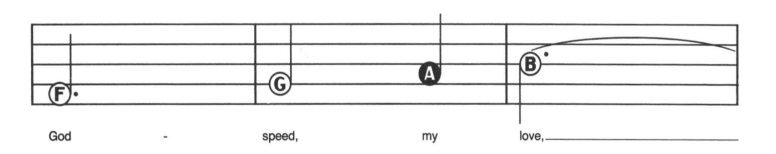

God - speed,   my   love,_____

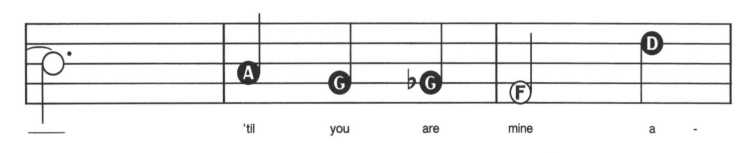

_____   'til   you   are   mine   a -

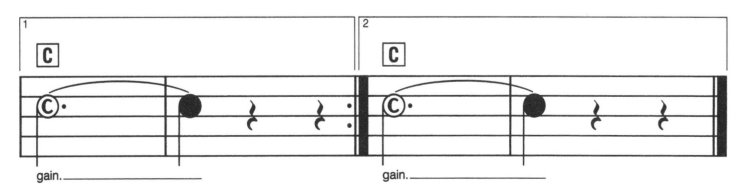

gain._____   gain._____

Speak Softly, Love
(Love Theme)
from the Paramount Picture THE GODFATHER

Registration 1
Rhythm: Ballad or Slow Rock

Words by Larry Kusik
Music by Nino Rota

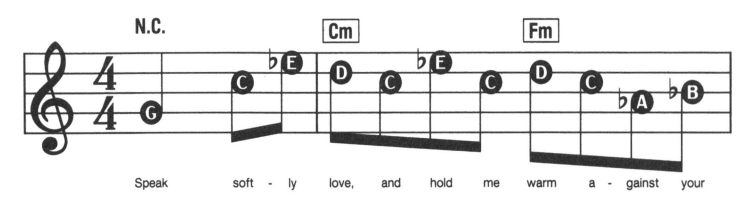

Speak soft - ly love, and hold me warm a - gainst your

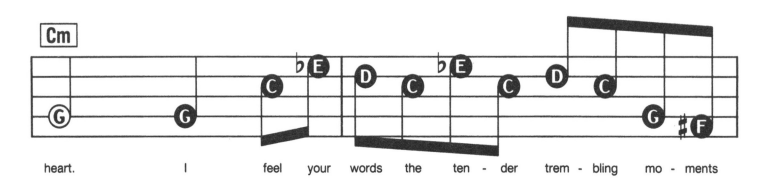

heart. I feel your words the ten - der trem - bling mo - ments

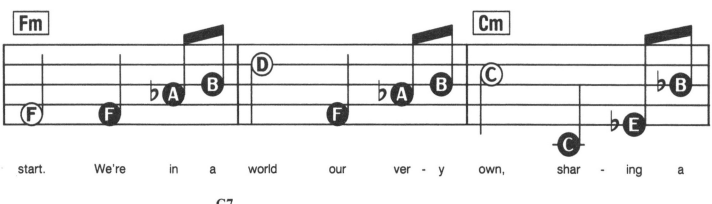

start. We're in a world our ver - y own, shar - ing a

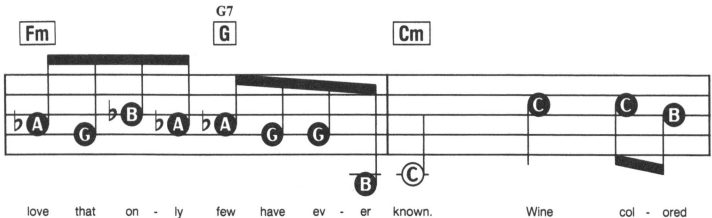

love that on - ly few have ev - er known. Wine col - ored

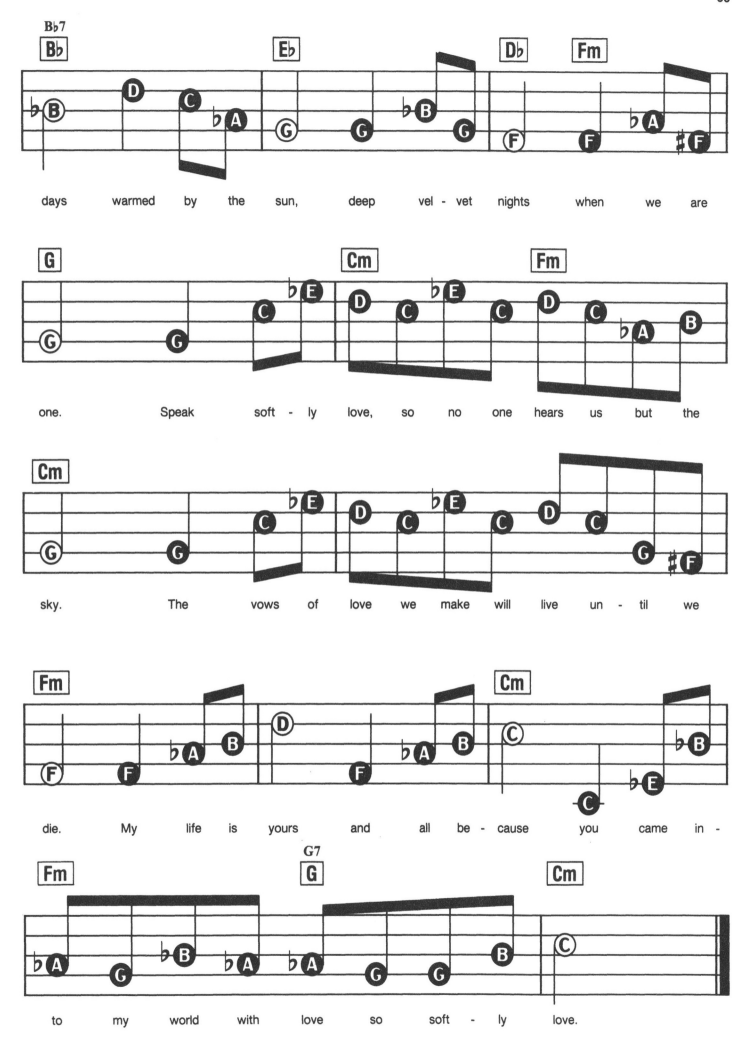

The Sweetheart Tree
from THE GREAT RACE

Registration 2
Rhythm: Waltz

Words by Johnny Mercer
Music by Henry Mancini

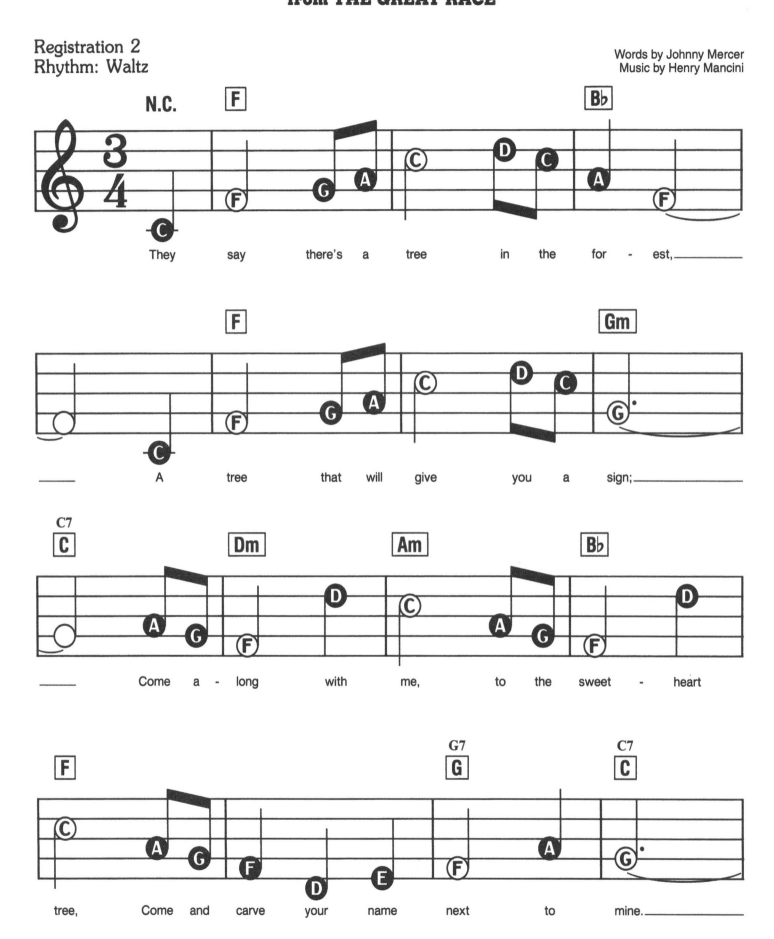

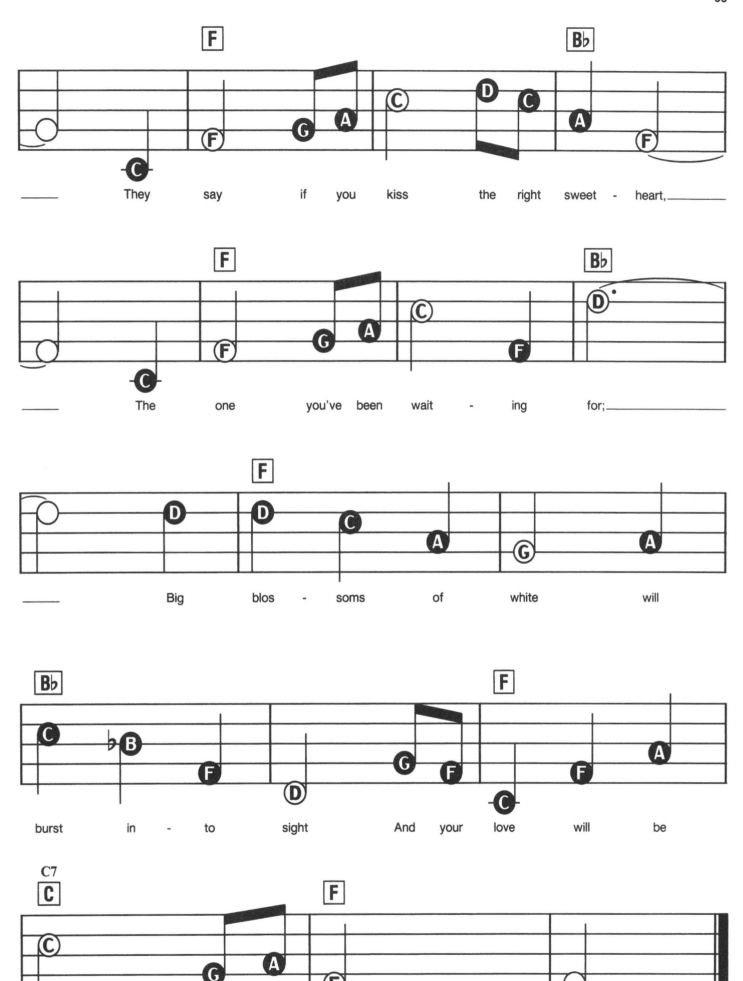

Talk to the Animals
from DOCTOR DOOLITTLE

Registration 4
Rhythm: Swing

Words and Music by
Leslie Bricusse

N.C.

Dm **Bb**

C D E | F F E | F E D

If we could talk to the an - i - mals,
talk to the an - i - mals,
ferred with our fur - ry friends,

G **C**

F G F E D | E #D E F

just im - a - gine it, chat - ting to a
learn their lan - gua - ges, may - be take an
man to an - i - mal, think of all the

C **G7 G** **C** **Am** To Coda ⊕

G E G C G | C D E

chimp in chim - pan - zee. Im - a - gine
an - i - mal de - gree, we'd stud - y
things we could dis - cuss. If we could

Dm **Bb** **G7 G** **C**

F E F E F D | G #F G #F

talk - ing to a tig - er, chat - ting to a
el - e - phant and ea - gle, buf - fa - lo and

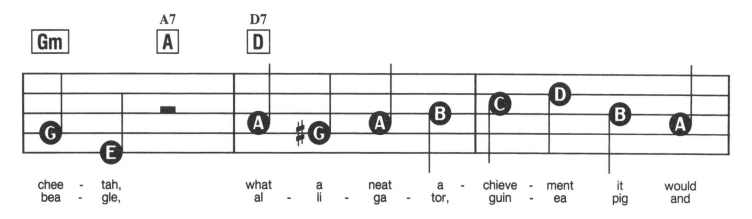

cheetah, what a neat a-chieve-ment it would

beagle, al-li-ga-tor, guin-ea pig and

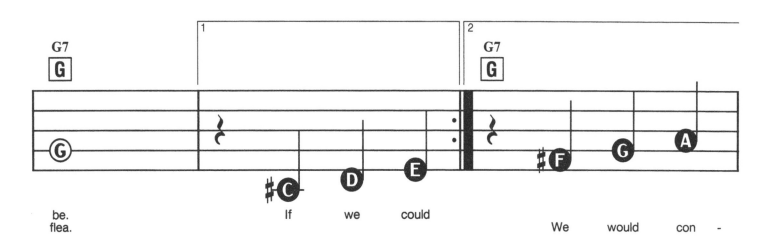

be. If we could

flea. We would con -

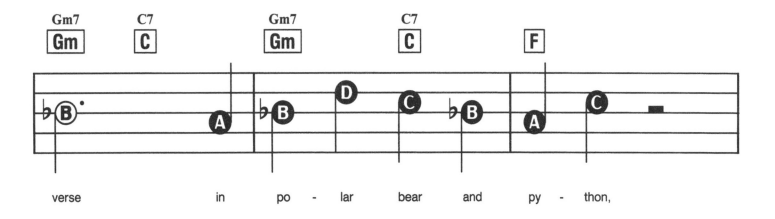

verse in po-lar bear and py-thon,

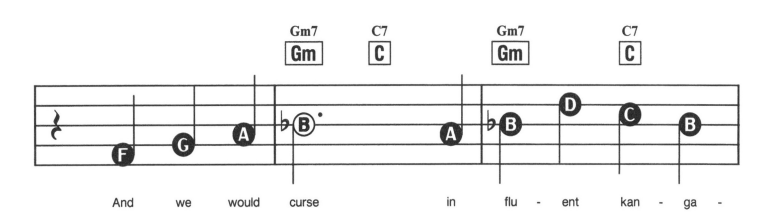

And we would curse in flu-ent kan-ga -

58

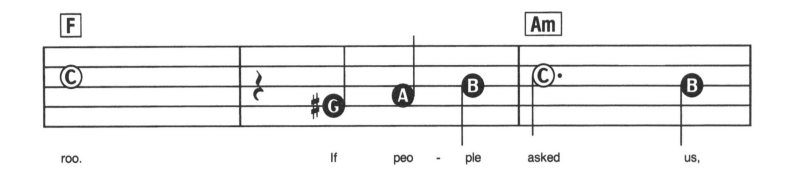

roo.   If   peo - ple asked   us,

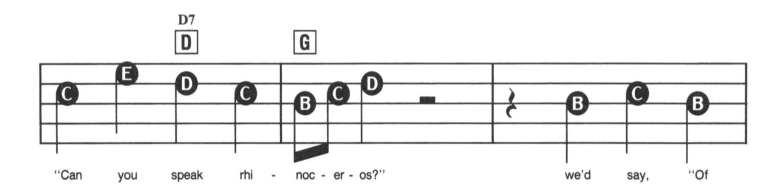

"Can   you   speak rhi - noc - er - os?"   we'd say, "Of

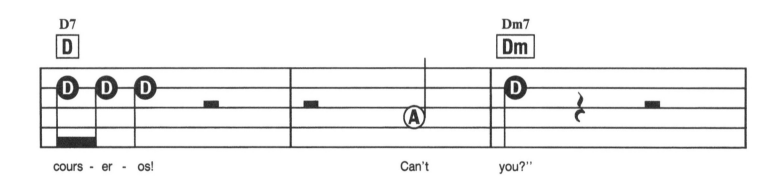

cours - er - os!   Can't   you?"

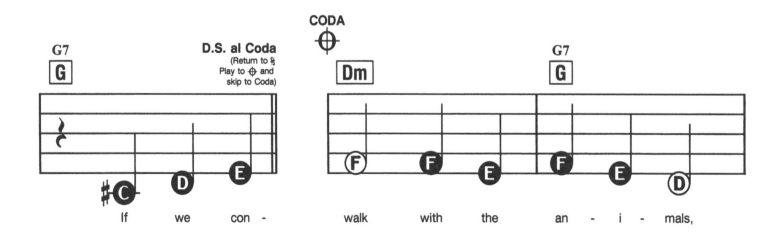

If we con -   walk with the   an - i - mals,

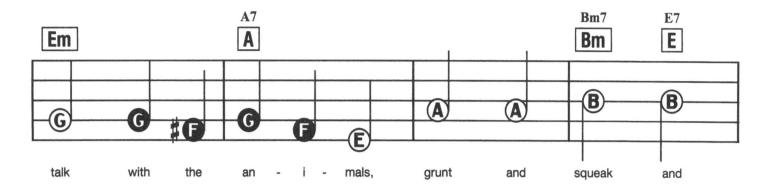

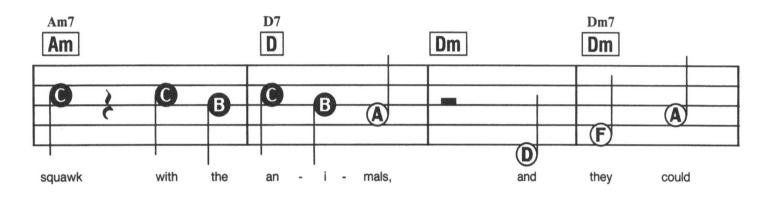

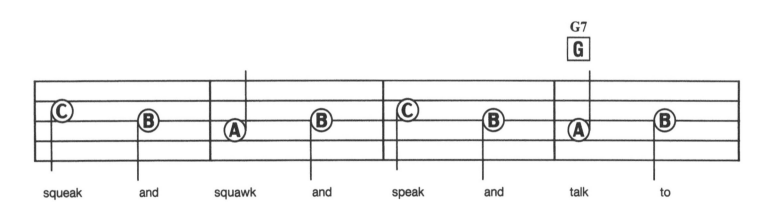

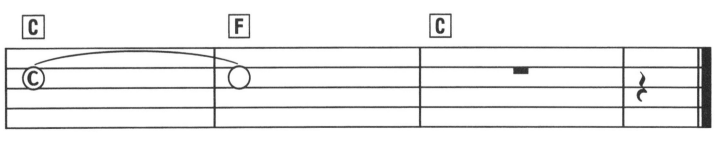

That's Amore

(That's Love)

from the Paramount Picture THE CADDY

Registration 3
Rhythm: Waltz

Words by Jack Brooks
Music by Harry Warren

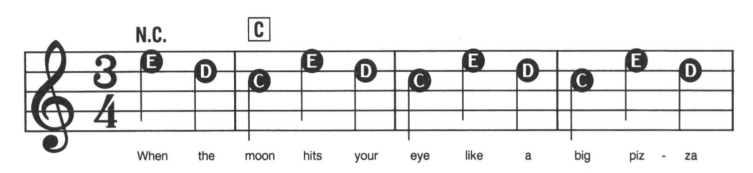

When the moon hits your eye like a big piz - za

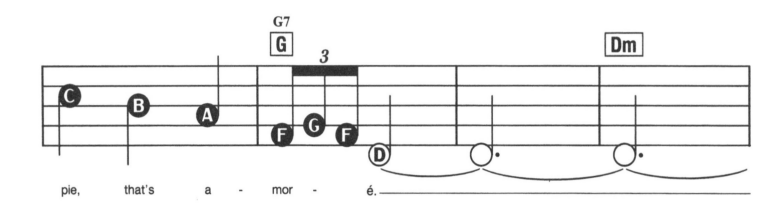

pie, that's a - mor - é. _____

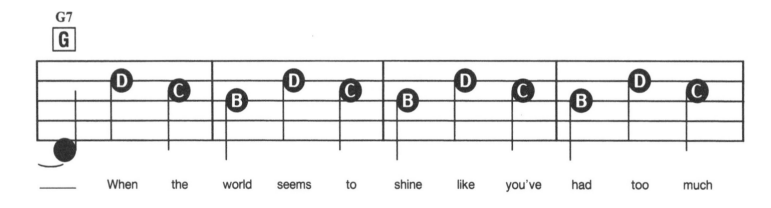

_____ When the world seems to shine like you've had too much

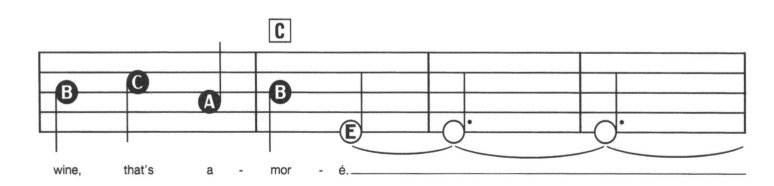

wine, that's a - mor - é. _____

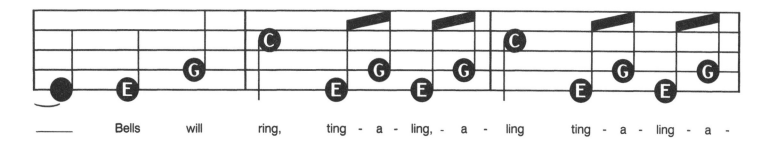

_____ Bells will ring, ting - a - ling, - a - ling ting - a - ling - a -

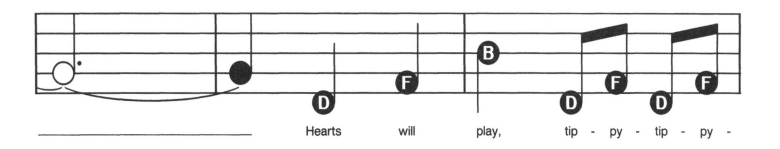

ling, and you'll sing, "Vee - ta bel - la." _____

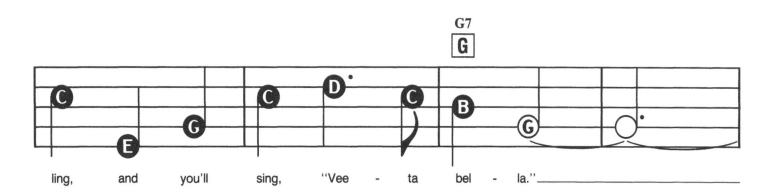

_____ Hearts will play, tip - py - tip - py -

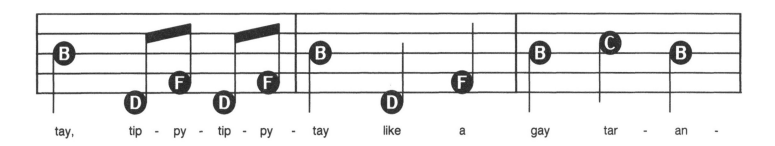

tay, tip - py - tip - py - tay like a gay tar - an -

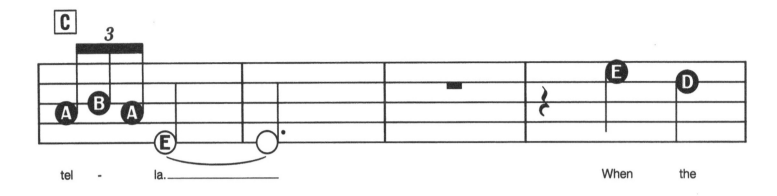

tel - la._____ When the

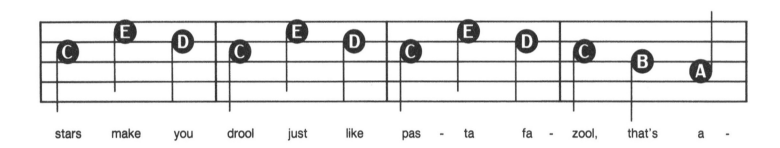

stars make you drool just like pas - ta fa - zool, that's a -

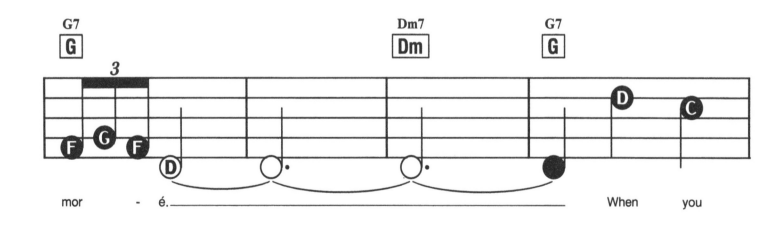

mor - é._____ When you

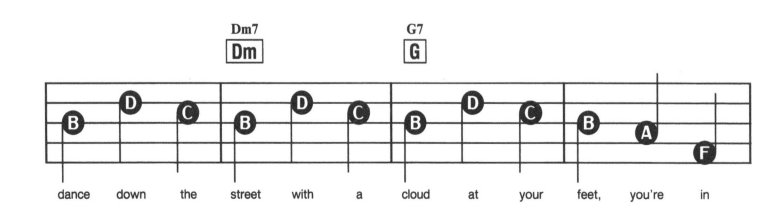

dance down the street with a cloud at your feet, you're in

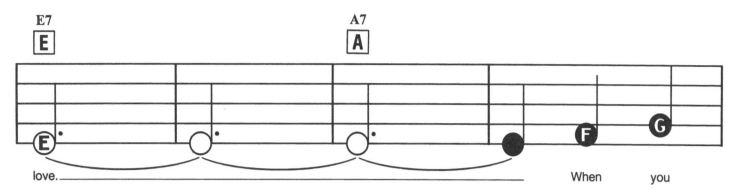

love. When you

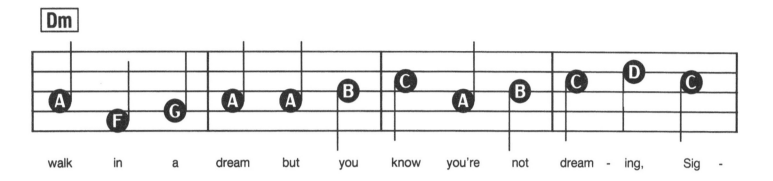

walk in a dream but you know you're not dream - ing, Sig -

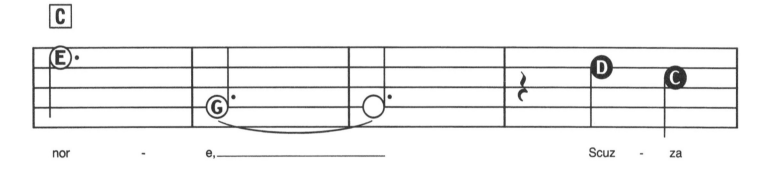

nor - e, Scuz - za

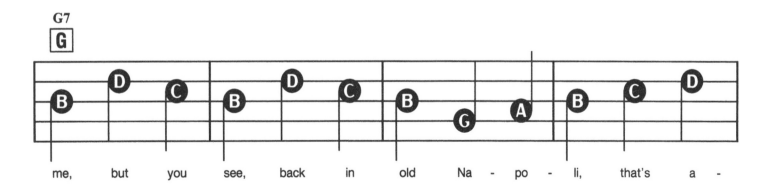

me, but you see, back in old Na - po - li, that's a -

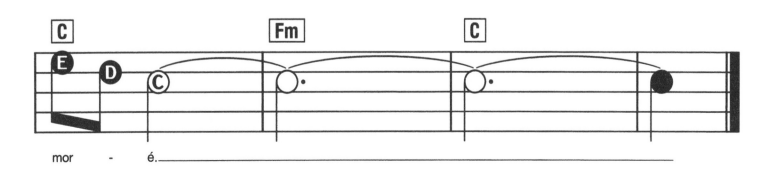

mor - é.

A Time for Us
(Love Theme)
from the Paramount Picture ROMEO AND JULIET

Registration 1
Rhythm: Waltz

Words by Larry Kusik and Eddie Snyder
Music by Nino Rota

Thanks for the Memory

from the Paramount Picture BIG BROADCAST OF 1938

Registration 3
Rhythm: Swing

Words and Music by Leo Robin
and Ralph Rainger

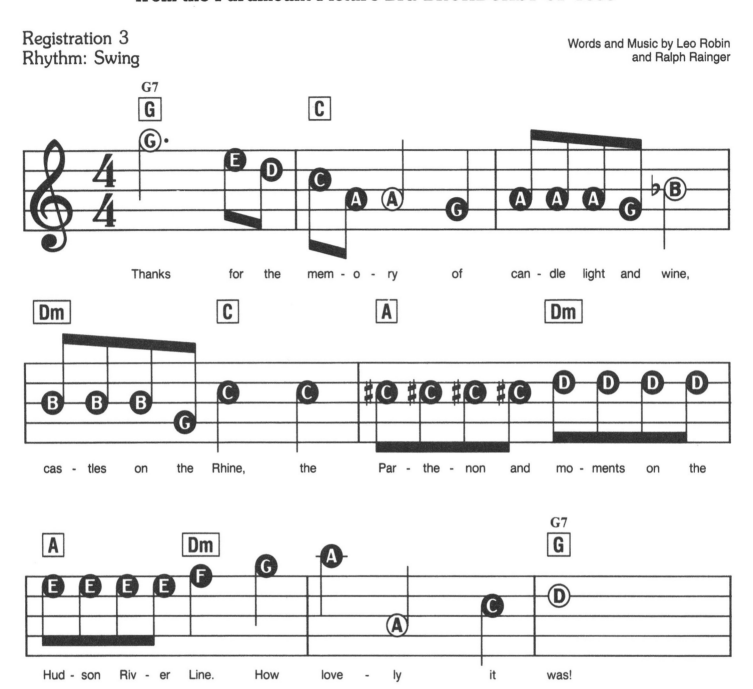

Thanks for the mem - o - ry of can - dle light and wine, cas - tles on the Rhine, the Par - the - non and mo - ments on the Hud - son Riv - er Line. How love - ly it was!

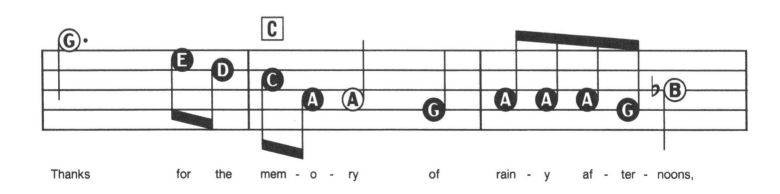

Thanks for the mem - o - ry of rain - y af - ter - noons,

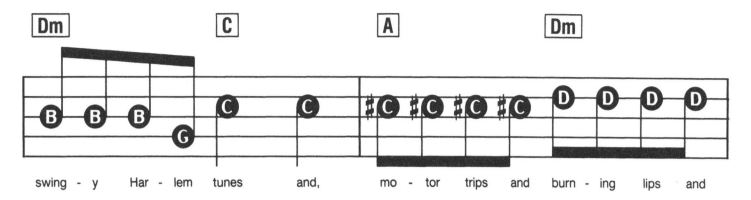

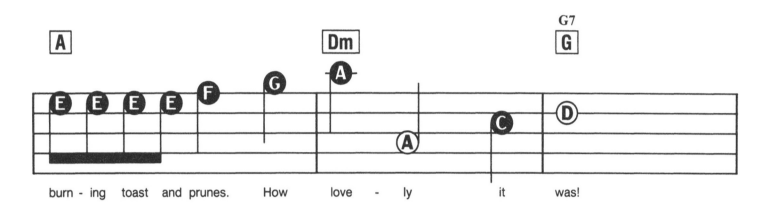

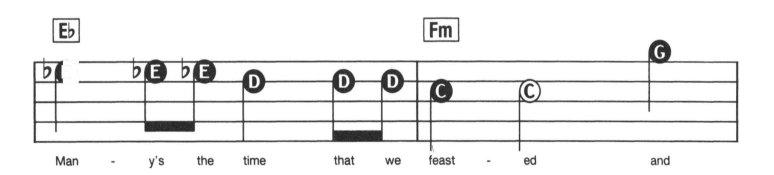

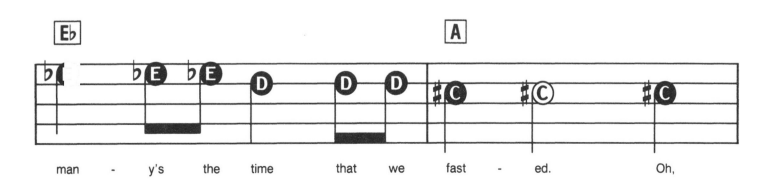

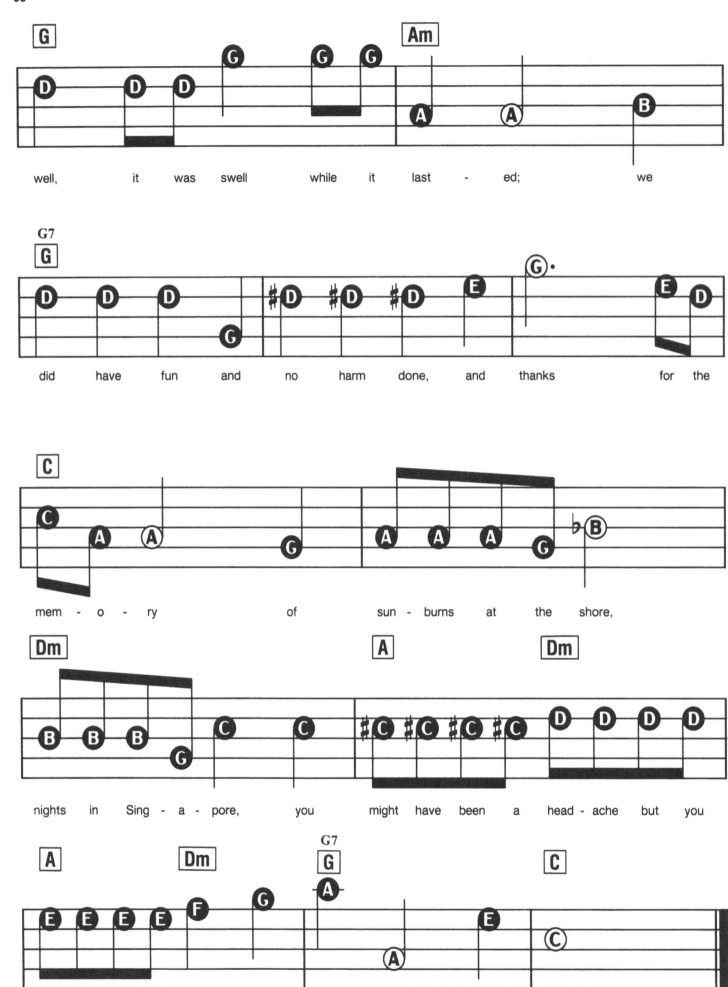

We're Off to See the Wizard
from THE WIZARD OF OZ

Registration 2
Rhythm: Waltz

Lyric by E.Y. Harburg
Music by Harold Arlen

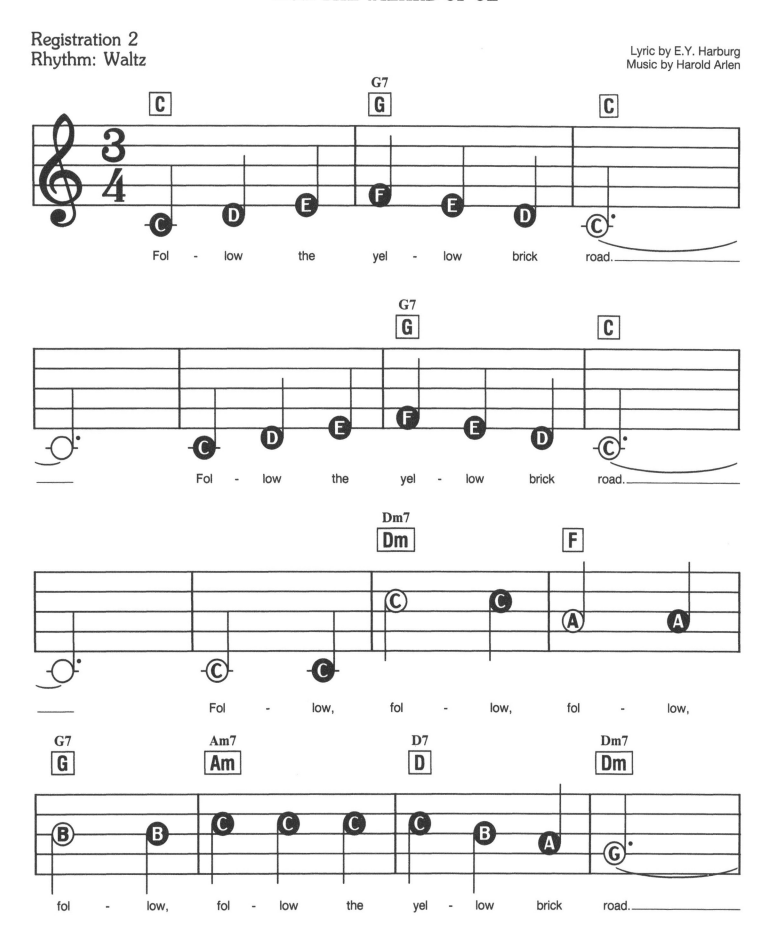

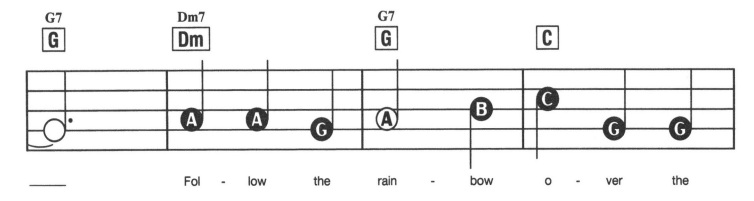

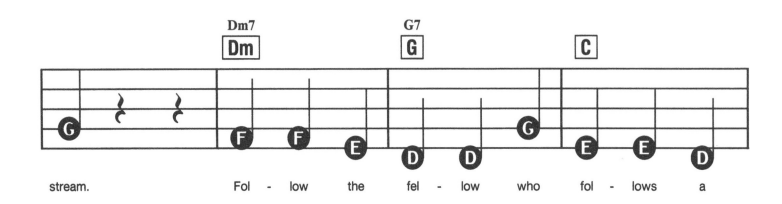

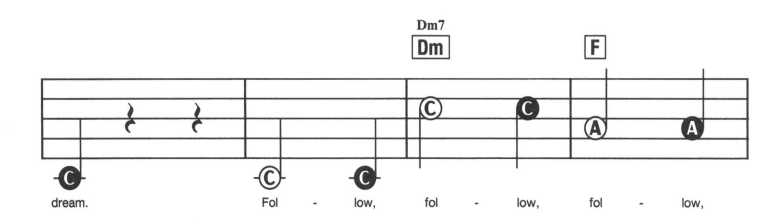

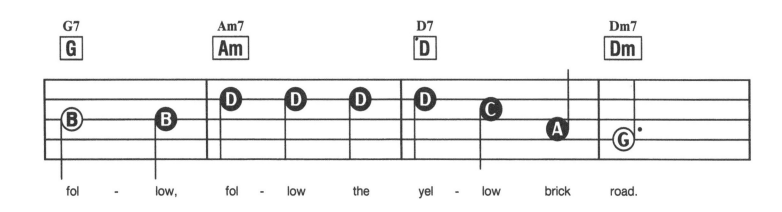

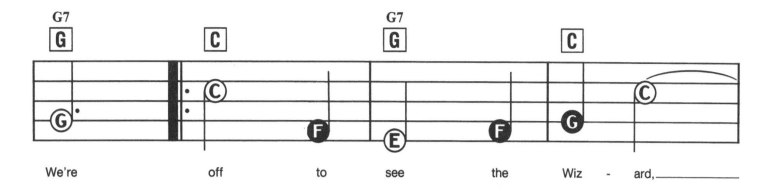

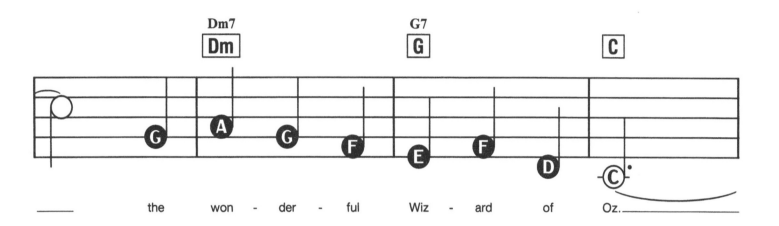

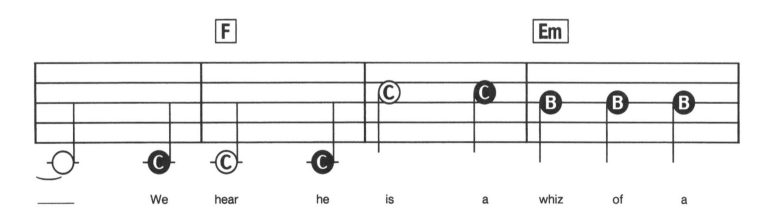

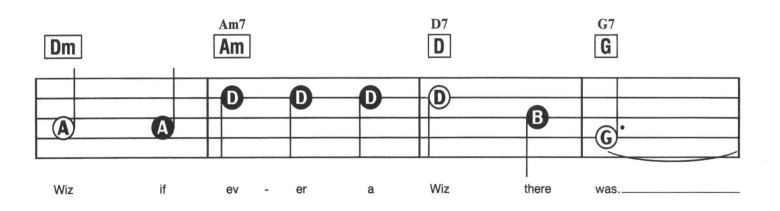

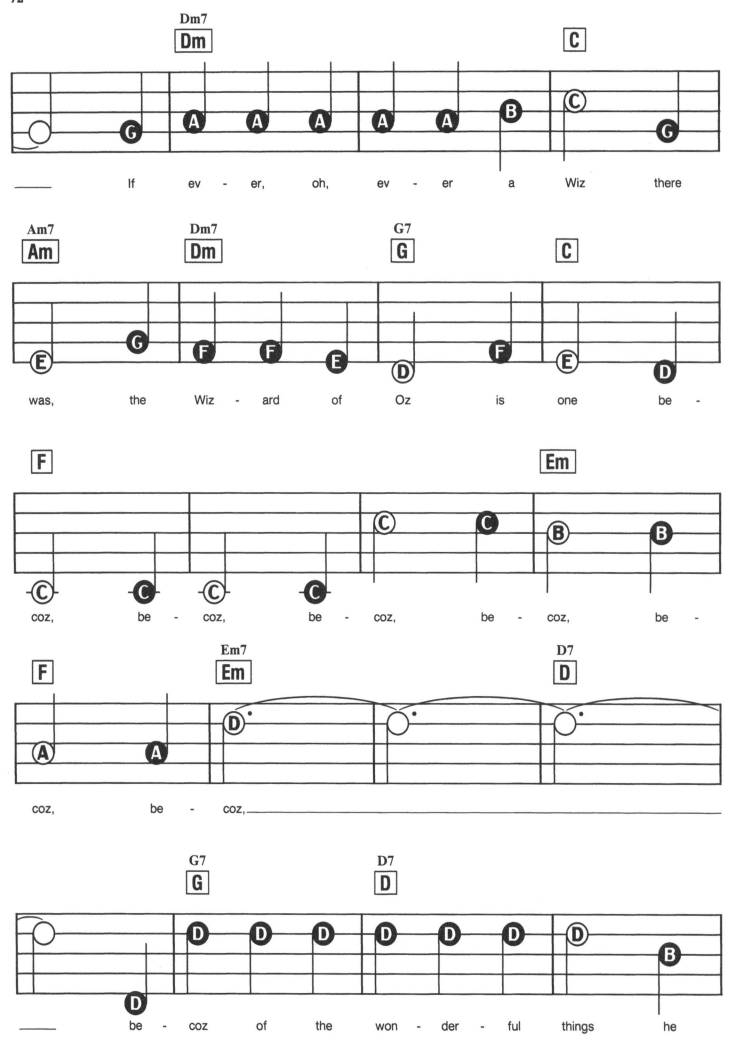

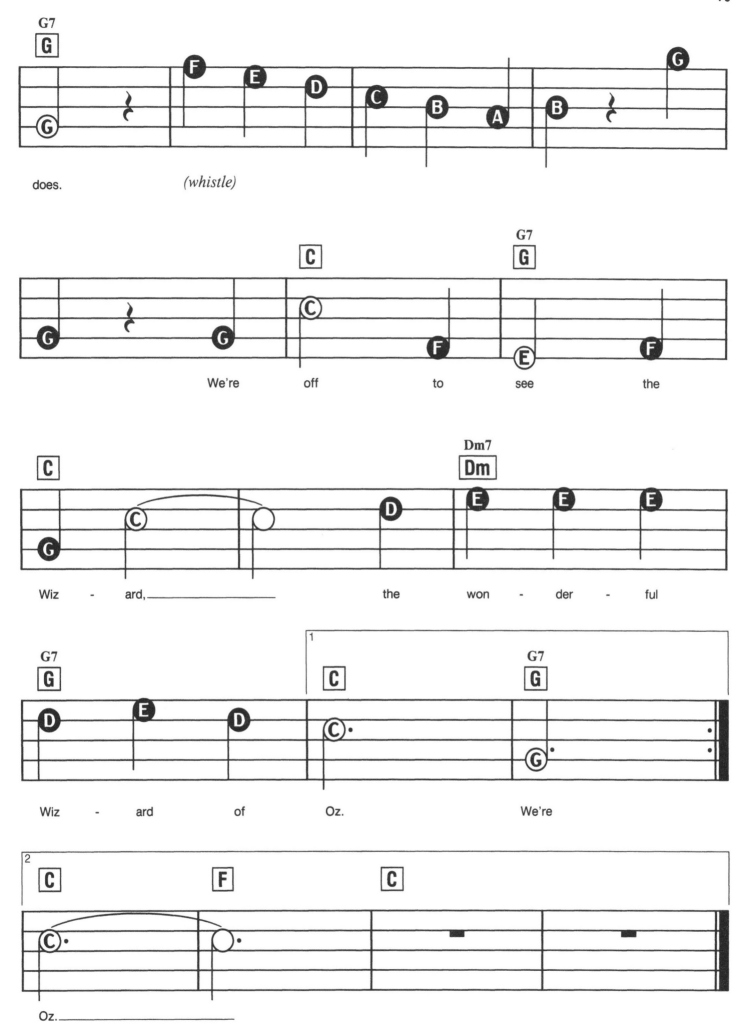

The Way We Were
from the Motion Picture THE WAY WE WERE

Registration 8
Rhythm: Pops or Rock

Words by Alan and Marilyn Bergman
Music by Marvin Hamlisch

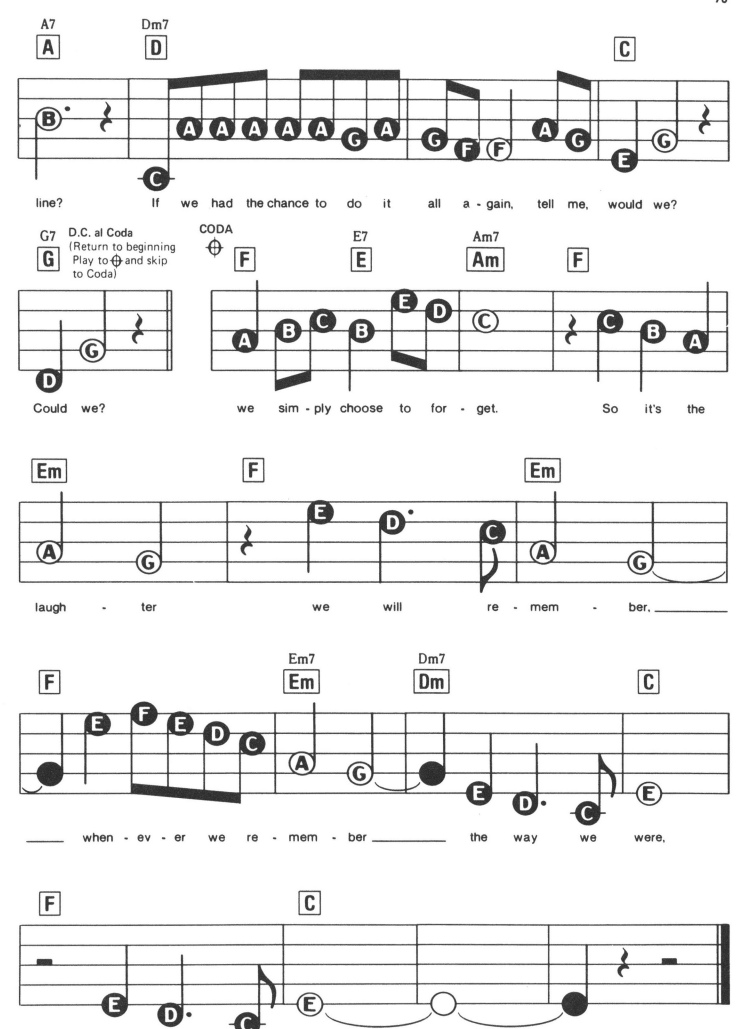

What Are You Doing the Rest of Your Life?

from THE HAPPY ENDING

Registration 2
Rhythm: Bossa Nova or Rock

Lyrics by Alan and Marilyn Bergman
Music by Michel Legrand

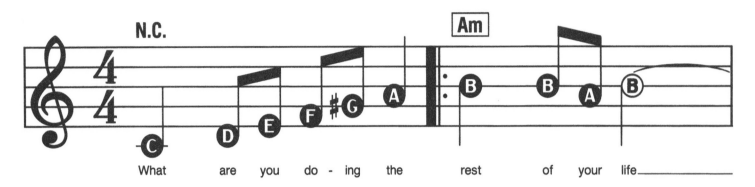

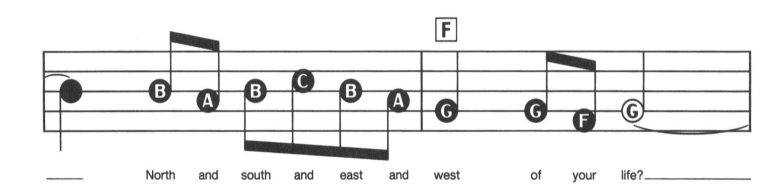

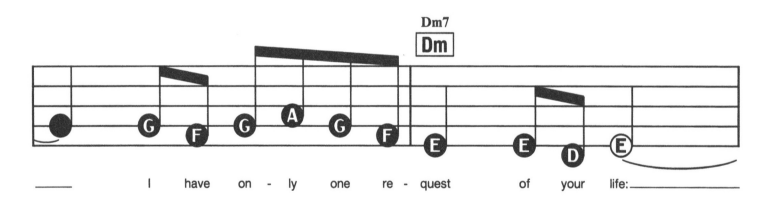

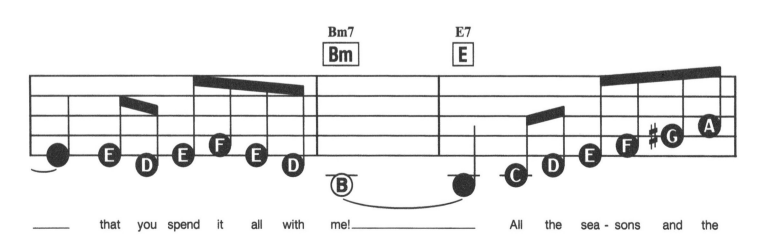

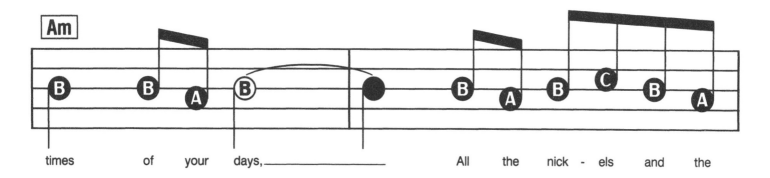

times of your days,_____ All the nick-els and the

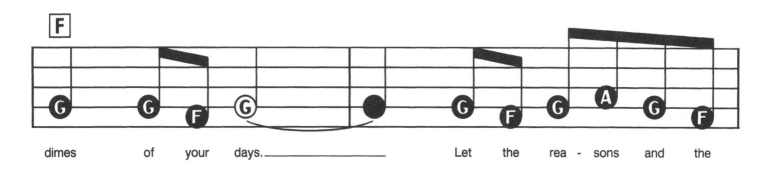

dimes of your days._____ Let the rea-sons and the

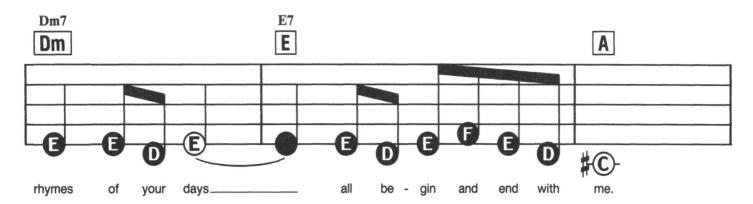

rhymes of your days_____ all be-gin and end with me.

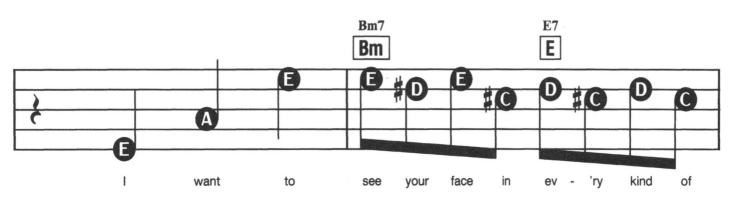

I want to see your face in ev-'ry kind of

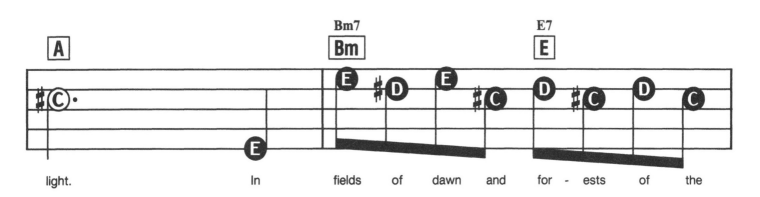

light. In fields of dawn and for-ests of the

It may take a kiss or two! _____ Thru

all of my life, _____ Sum - mer, win - ter, spring and

fall of my life, _____ All I ev - er will re -

call of my life is all of my life with

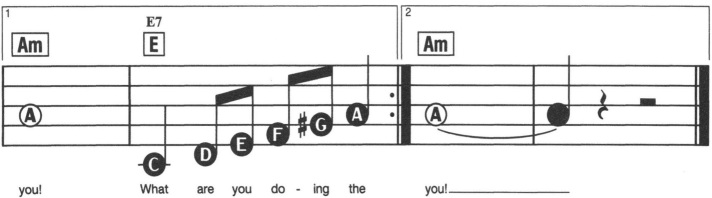

you! What are you do - ing the you! _____

Where Do I Begin
(Love Theme)
from the Paramount Picture LOVE STORY

Registration 8
Rhythm: Ballad or Slow Rock

Words by Carl Sigman
Music by Francis Lai

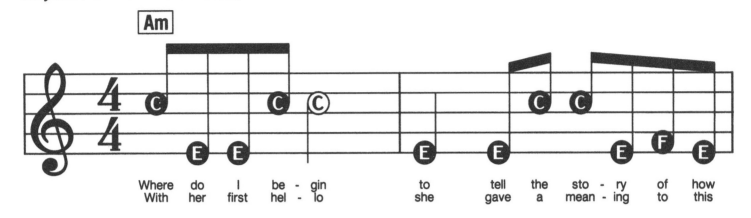

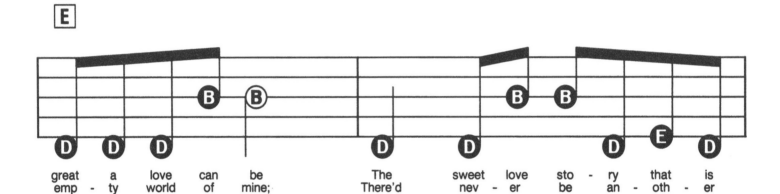

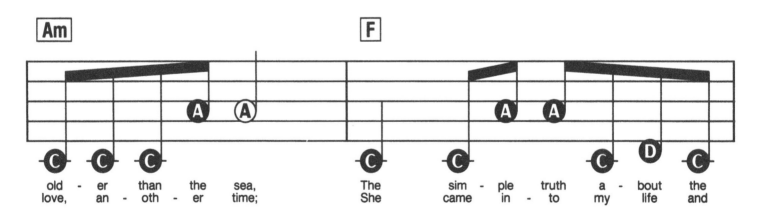

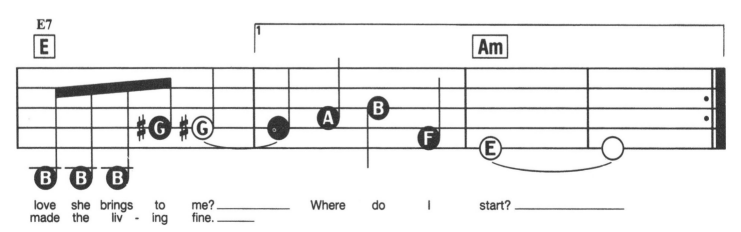

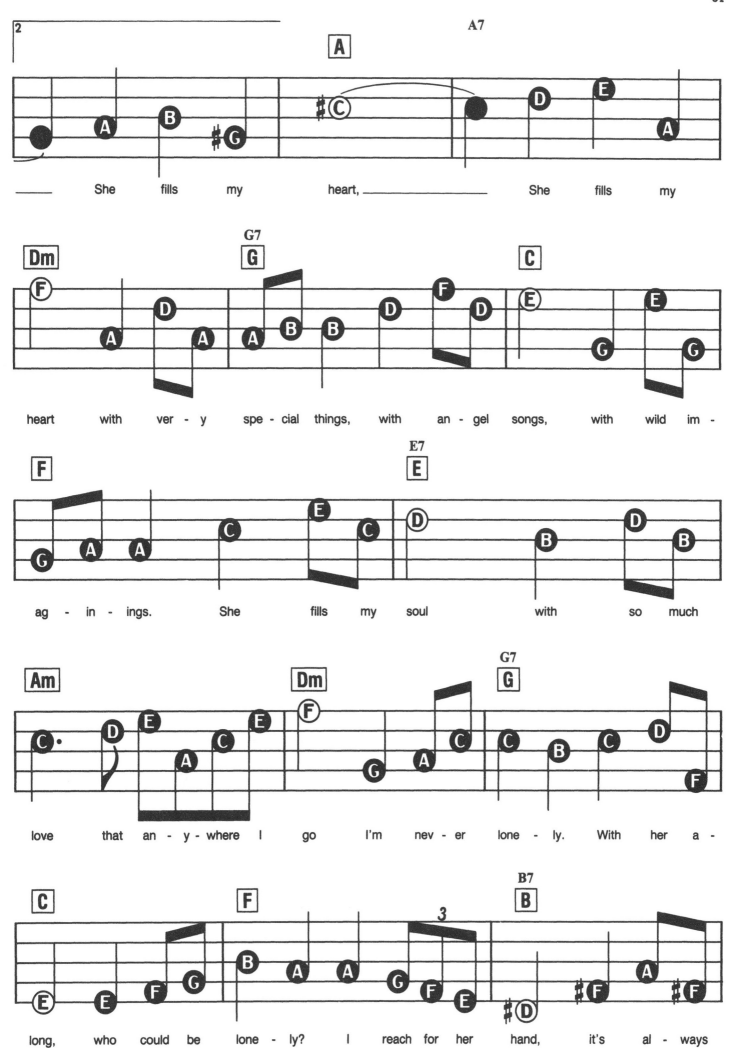

Where the Boys Are

featured in the Motion Picture WHERE THE BOYS ARE

Registration 3
Rhythm: Rock or 8 Beat

Words and Music by Howard Greenfield
and Neil Sedaka

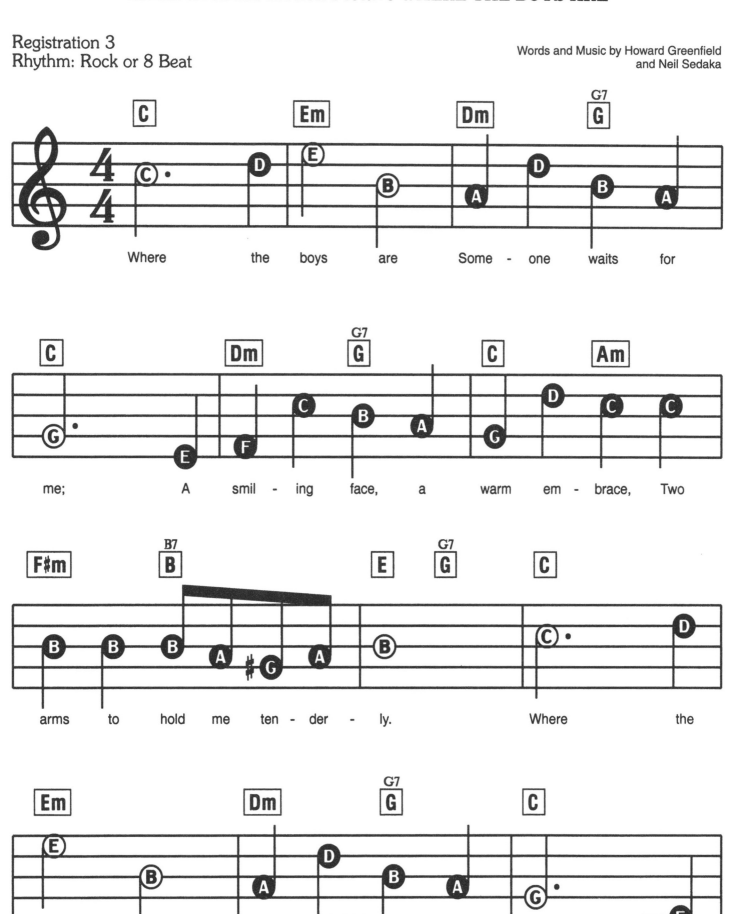

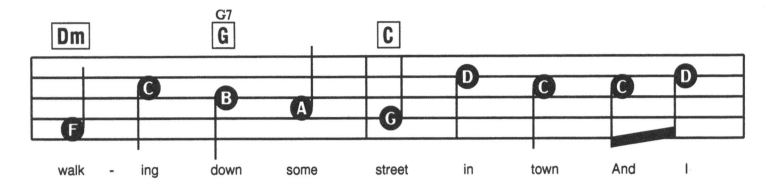

walk - ing down some street in town And I

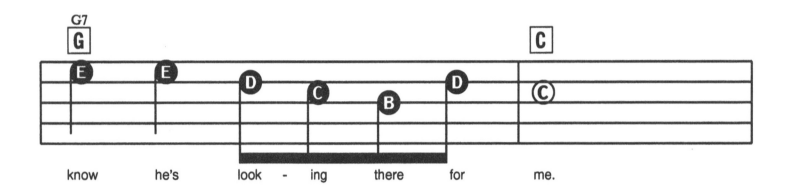

know he's look - ing there for me.

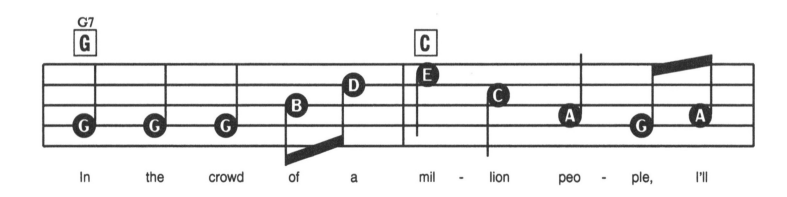

In the crowd of a mil - lion peo - ple, I'll

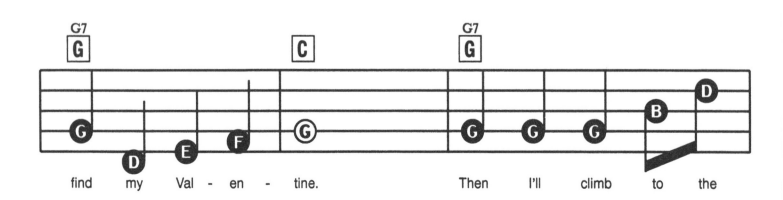

find my Val - en - tine. Then I'll climb to the

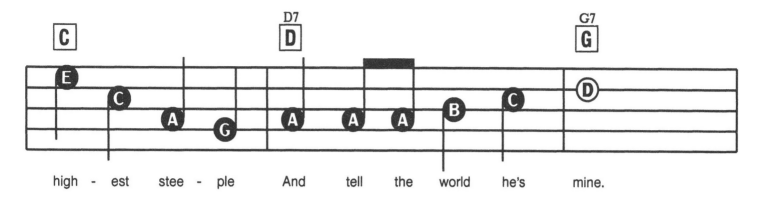

high - est stee - ple   And   tell   the   world   he's   mine.

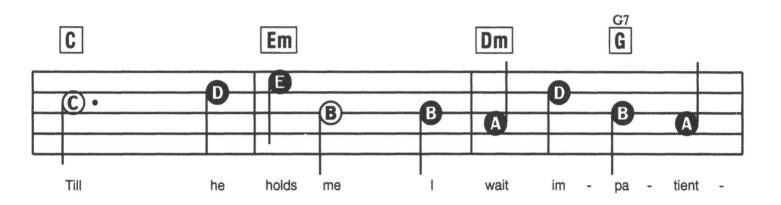

Till   he   holds   me   I   wait   im - pa - tient -

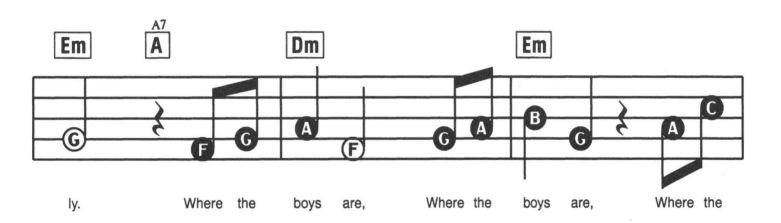

ly.   Where the   boys   are,   Where the   boys   are,   Where the

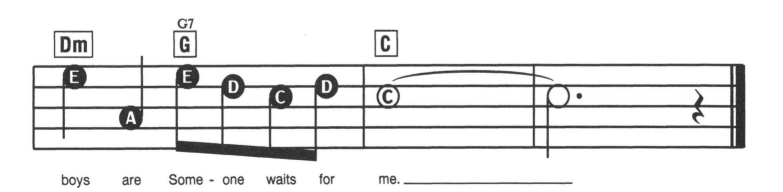

boys   are   Some - one   waits   for   me. _____

Where Is Your Heart
(The Song from Moulin Rouge)
from MOULIN ROUGE

Registration 2
Rhythm: Waltz

Words by William Engvick
Music by George Auric

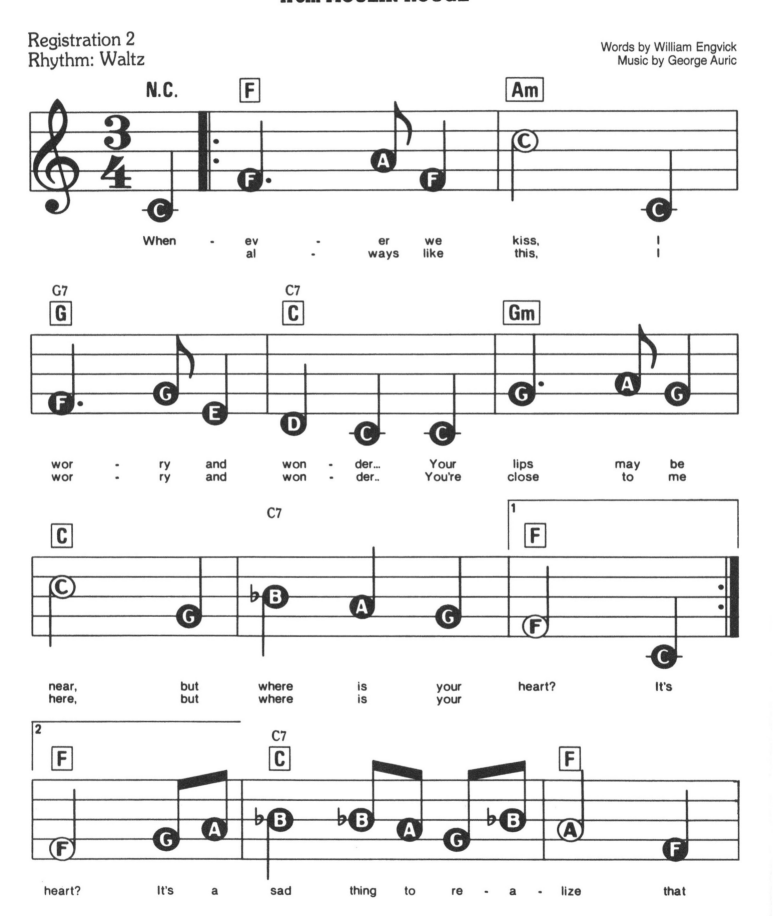

The Windmills of Your Mind

Theme from THE THOMAS CROWN AFFAIR

Registration 2
Rhythm: Rock or 8 Beat

Lyrics by Alan and Marilyn Bergman
Music by Michel Legrand

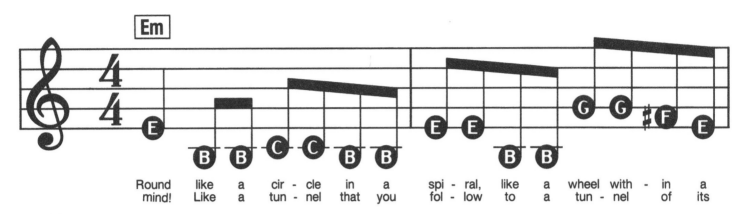

Round like a cir - cle in a spi - ral, like a wheel with - in a
mind! Like a tun - nel that you fol - low to a tun - nel of its

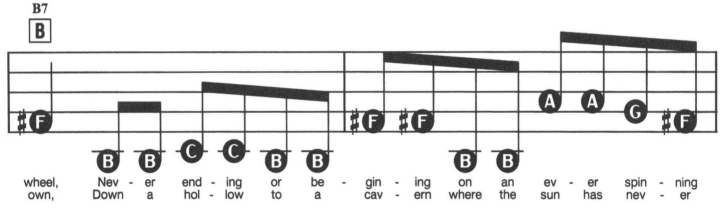

wheel, Nev - er end - ing or be - gin - ing on an ev - er spin - ning
own, Down a hol - low to a cav - ern where the sun has nev - er

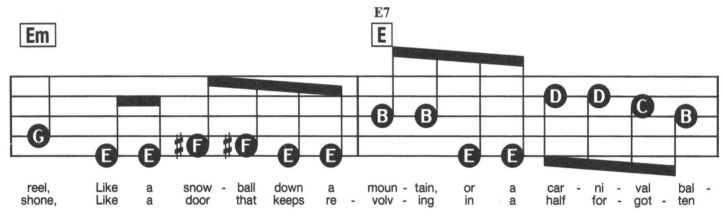

reel, Like a snow - ball down a moun - tain, or a car - ni - val bal -
shone, Like a door that keeps re - volv - ing in a half for - got - ten

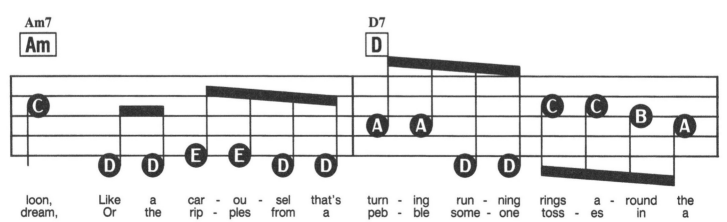

loon, Like a car - ou - sel that's turn - ing run - ning rings a - round the
dream, Or the rip - ples from a peb - ble some - one toss - es in a

89

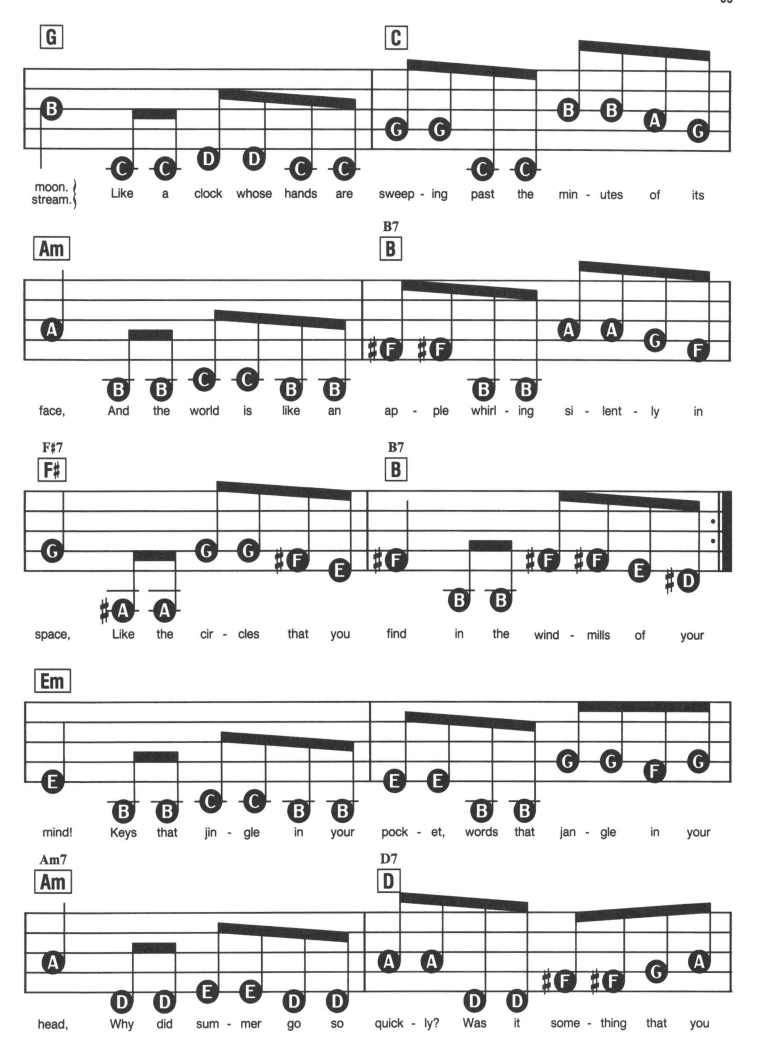

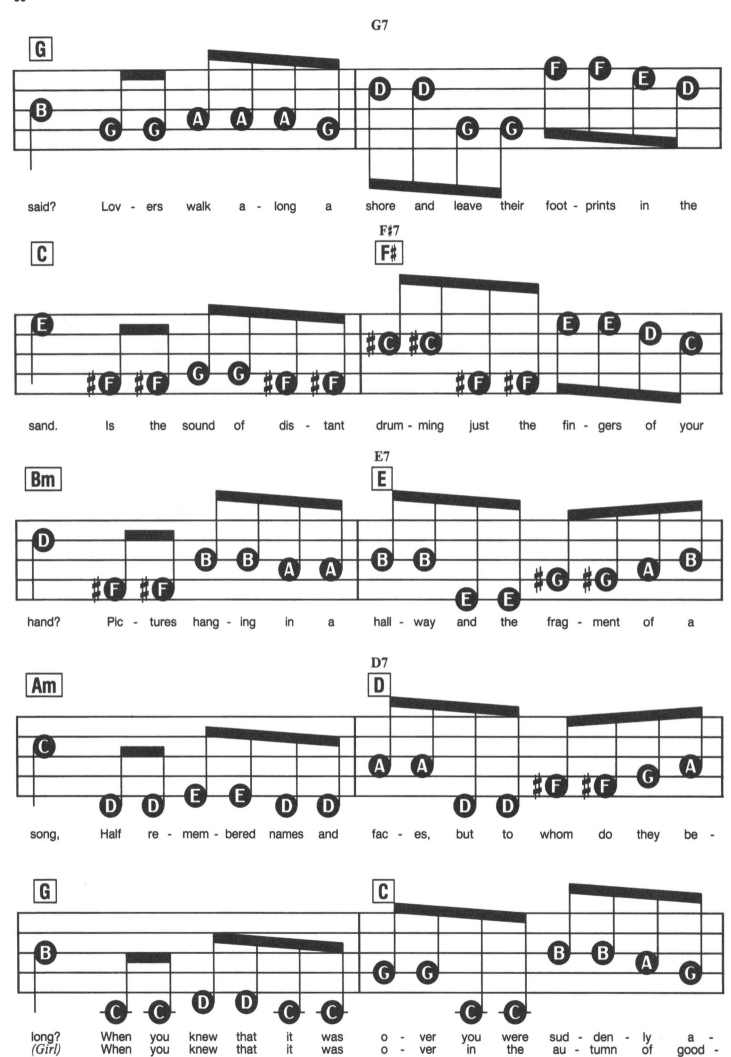

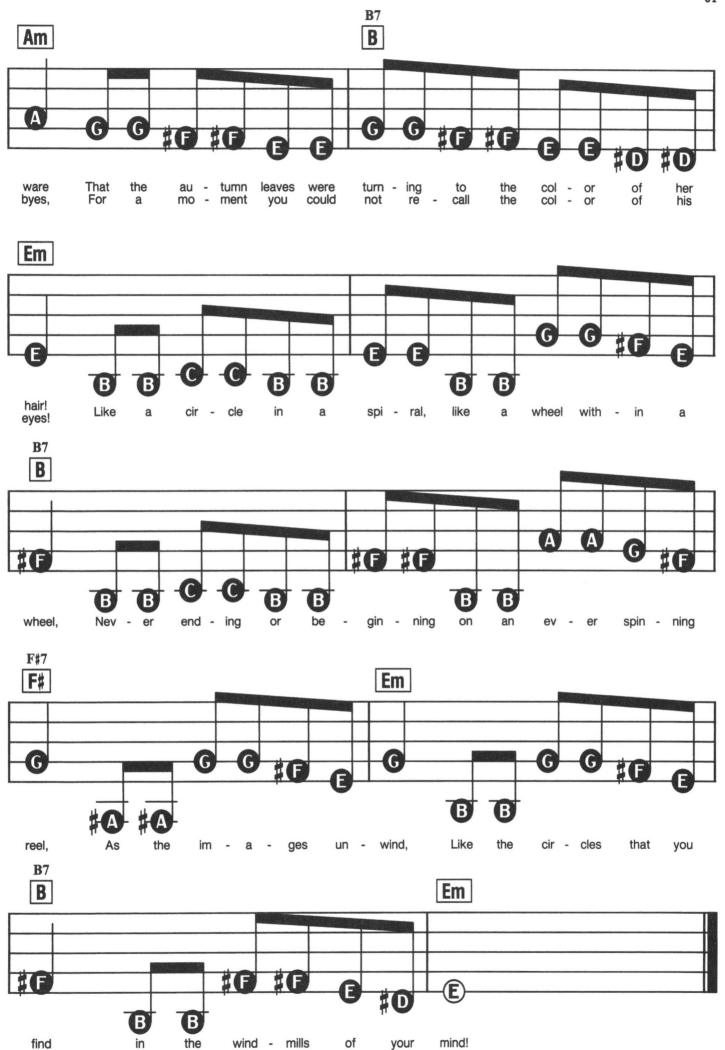

You Light Up My Life

from YOU LIGHT UP MY LIFE

Words and Music by
Joe Brooks

Registration 7
Rhythm: Waltz

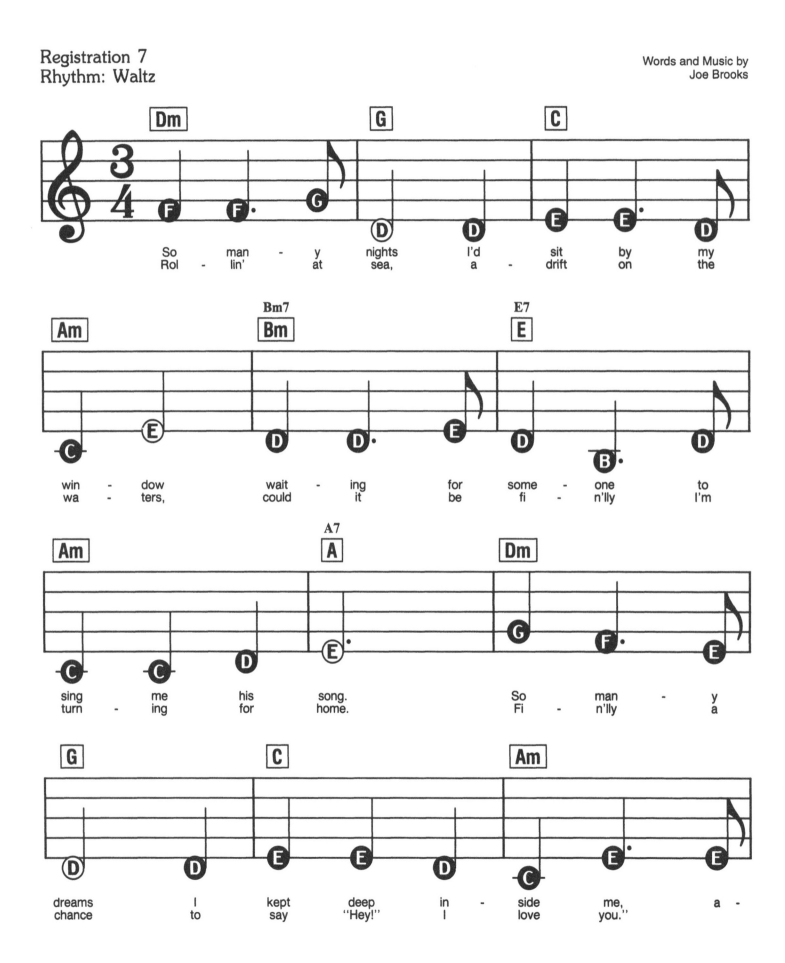

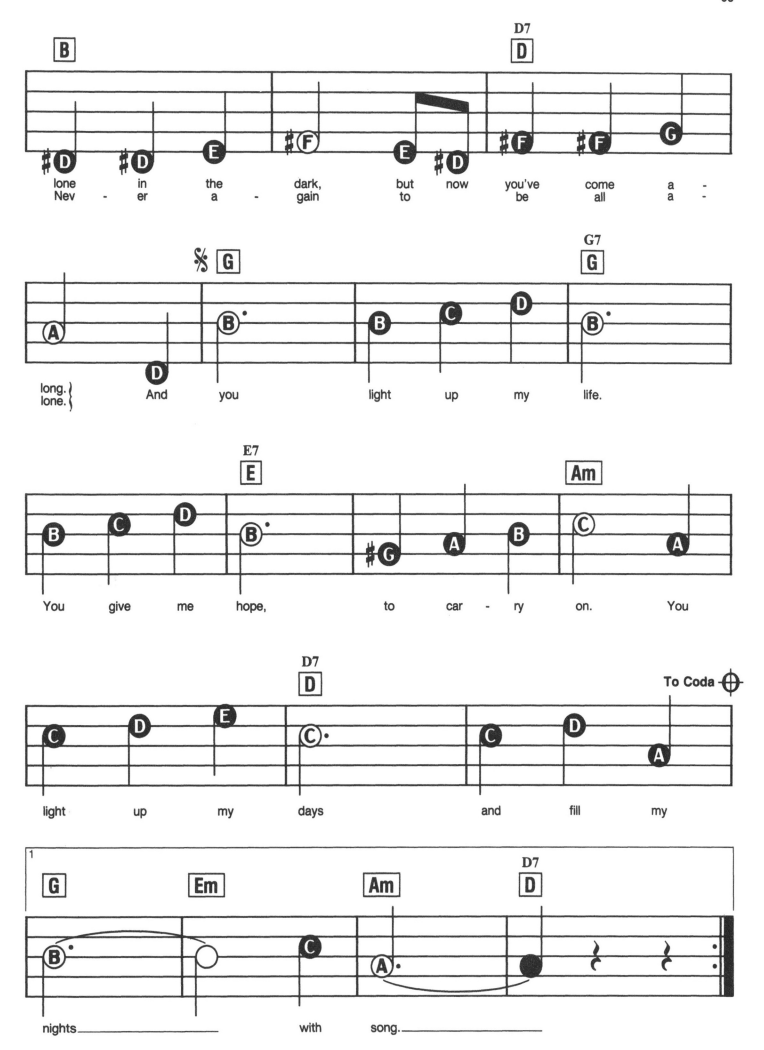

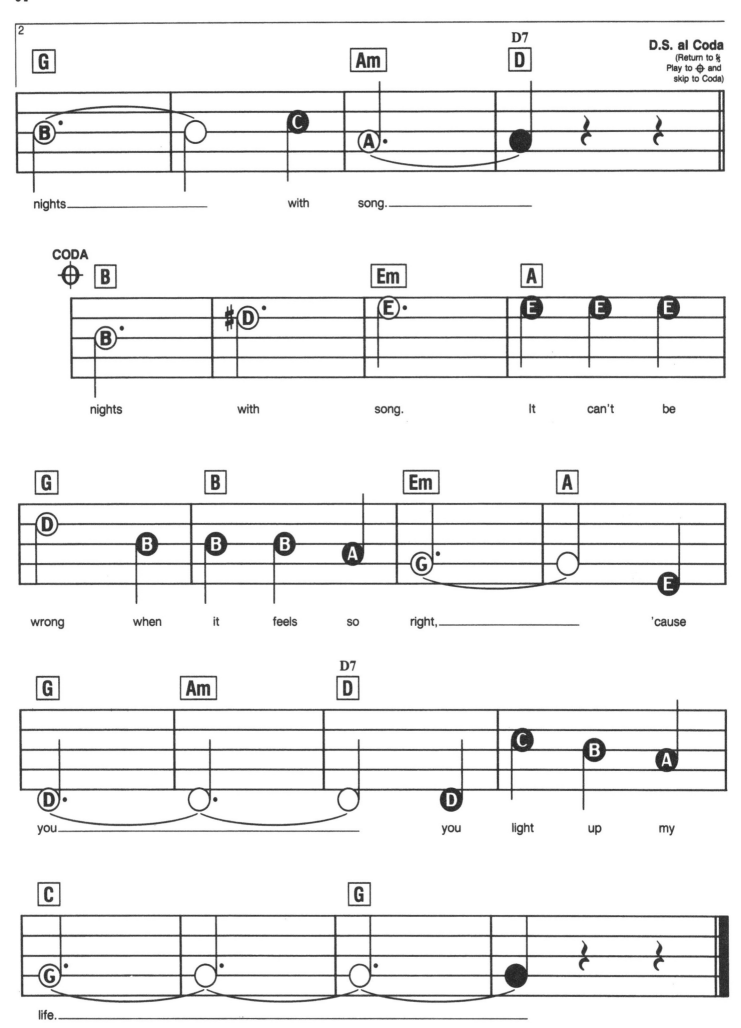

Registration Guide

• Match the Registration number on the song to the corresponding numbered category below. Select and activate an instrumental sound available on your instrument.

• Choose an automatic rhythm appropriate to the mood and style of the song. (Consult your Owner's Guide for proper operation of automatic rhythm features.)

• Adjust the tempo and volume controls to comfortable settings.

Registration

1	Mellow	Flutes, Clarinet, Oboe, Flugel Horn, Trombone, French Horn, Organ Flutes
2	Ensemble	Brass Section, Sax Section, Wind Ensemble, Full Organ, Theater Organ
3	Strings	Violin, Viola, Cello, Fiddle, String Ensemble, Pizzicato, Organ Strings
4	Guitars	Acoustic/Electric Guitars, Banjo, Mandolin, Dulcimer, Ukulele, Hawaiian Guitar
5	Mallets	Vibraphone, Marimba, Xylophone, Steel Drums, Bells, Celesta, Chimes
6	Liturgical	Pipe Organ, Hand Bells, Vocal Ensemble, Choir, Organ Flutes
7	Bright	Saxophones, Trumpet, Mute Trumpet, Synth Leads, Jazz/Gospel Organs
8	Piano	Piano, Electric Piano, Honky Tonk Piano, Harpsichord, Clavi
9	Novelty	Melodic Percussion, Wah Trumpet, Synth, Whistle, Kazoo, Perc. Organ
10	Bellows	Accordion, French Accordion, Mussette, Harmonica, Pump Organ, Bagpipes